William Edward Brown

A HISTORY OF
SEVENTEENTH-CENTURY
RUSSIAN LITERATURE

ARDIS ≅ ≅ ≅ ANN ARBOR

Library of Congress Cataloging in Publication Data

Brown, William Edward, 1904-
   A history of seventeenth-century Russian literature.

   Bibliography: p.
   Includes index.
   1. Russian literature—17th century—History and criticism.
I. Title.
PG3002.B7   891.7'09'001   79-21979
ISBN 0-88233-343-7

Published by Ardis,
2901 Heatherway,
Ann Arbor, Michigan, 48104

Manufactured by Lakeland Press, Dexter, Michigan

For Ralph and Frances

FOREWORD

I undertook a study of this period when it became clear to me that the splendid literature of Russia's eighteenth century was scarcely intelligible without reference to its beginnings in the century before. I thought of the study at first as little more than a prelude to a comprehensive volume on the eighteenth century; but as it developed, it seemed better to separate the two and give the seventeenth century an independent, if small, treatment of its own.

Few seventeenth-century Russian works are of such outstanding literary merit as to justify extensive treatment or quotation. In any case, complete works from the age are seldom available in accessible modern editions, but are likely to be buried in pre-Soviet historical and antiquarian journals. I have had, for better or worse, to rely in most cases on anthologies. Anthologized extracts are often unsatisfactory, but have the merit of presenting at least an inclusive general view of a work or author. I do not think that in the present case much has been lost by this procedure.

English translations of Russian literature of the seventeenth century are virtually nonexistent. An exception is the *Life of the Archpriest Avvakum, Written by Himself*, which was translated by Jane Harrison and Hope Mirrless, published in 1924 by Hogarth Press, London, and reprinted in 1963 by Archon Books (The Shoe String Press, Inc., Hampden, Conn.), by whose kind permission I have used this translation for quotations, in Serge Zenkovsky's slightly modernized version. All other translations used in the text are my own.

In the course of writing this book I have had the much appreciated assistance of Messrs. Clyde Haselden and Robert Gennett, of the David Bishop Skillman Library of Lafayette College, and I would like also to acknowledge my great indebtedness to Mr. Fred Moody, of the Ardis staff, for his extremely careful and intelligent handling of a difficult manuscript.

Grafton, Vermont   *William Edward Brown*
August 1979

CONTENTS

I. PROSE GENRES OF MEDIEVAL TYPE IN SEVENTEENTH-CENTURY RUSSIAN LITERATURE

Introduction and Generalities 3
The Historical Memoir 10
The Compilation 23
The Saint's Life 26

II. PROSE GENRES OF MODERN TYPE IN SEVENTEENTH-CENTURY RUSSIAN LITERATURE

Differentiation in Seventeenth-Century Russian Literature 37
The "Baroque" Period in Russian and Western Literature 38
The Exemplary Tale: "Savva Grudtsyn" 41
*The Historical Romance: "Tale of the Founding of the Page's
    Monastery"* 43
*The Chivalric Romance: "Bova Korolevich" and "Eruslan
    Lazarevich"* 45
The Picaresque Tale: "Frol Skobeev" 50
*The Satirical Tale: "Yorsh Yorshovich" and "Shemyaka's
    Judgment"* 54
*The Autobiography: "Life of Archpriest Avvakum, Written by
    Himself"* 61

III. POPULAR ORAL VERSE IN CONTACT WITH WRITTEN LITERATURE

Raeshnyi *and* Skomoroshnyi *Verse* 75
The Bylina 78
Lyric Verse: The Richard James and Kvashnin Collections 82
*The "Tale of Sorrow and Misfortune" ("Povest' o Gore i
    Zlochastii")* 87

IV. LEARNED OR BOOKISH POETRY IN THE SEVENTEENTH CENTURY

The Nature and Origins of "Syllabic" Verse 97
The Writers of Pre-Syllabic Verse 104
Writers of Syllabic Verse 109
    1. Simeon Polotsky 117

    2. Sylvester Medvedev **120**
    3. Karion Istomin **123**
    4. Dimitry Rostovsky **127**
    5. Stefan Yavorsky **127**
    6. Andrei Belobotsky **129**

V. SEVENTEENTH-CENTURY RUSSIAN DRAMA

The Beginnings **143**
The "Tragicomedy of Vladimir" of Feofan Prokopovich **150**

Conclusion 159

NOTES / BIBLIOGRAPHY / INDEX

Source Titles and Abbreviations Used in the Notes **165**
Notes **167**
Abbreviations Used in the Bibliography **171**
Bibliography: Russian Literature of the Seventeenth Century **173**

List of Illustrations

Page
    1 - Crown fashioned in 1627-28 for Tsar Mikhail Fyodorovich
    2 - The Terem Palace in the Kremlin, 1637
  34 - "The Tale of Bova Korolevich"
  35 - A popular print ("lubok") on a ribald theme
  36 - Title page of the "Life of St. Alexei"
between 55 and 56 - "The Tale of Yorsh Yorshevich"
  73 - Manuscript of Avvakum's autobiography
  74 - Patriarch Nikon
  94 - Manuscript copy of "The Tale of Sorrow-Misfortune"
  95 - Adam and Eve in the Bible in Pictures
  96 - 17th-century alphabet book
between 102-103 - Woodcuts showing "skomorokhi" and boyar dress
140 - Polotsky's "Comedy of the Prodigal Son"
141 - Simeon Polotsky and Pastor J. Gregory
142 - Inside Cathedral in Moscow's Novodevichi Monastery (17th cent.)
157 - Novodevichi Monastery, 1687-89
*158 - Ryabushkin painting of Muscovites watching foreigners enter
     Moscow*
161 - 17th-century icon of St. George and the Dragon
162 - St. Basil's Cathedral (from Olearius)

CHAPTER I

PROSE GENRES OF MEDIEVAL TYPE IN SEVENTEENTH CENTURY RUSSIAN LITERATURE

A. *Introduction and Generalities*

Russia's position in the world of European literature, just like Russia's position in the European political world, is an ambiguous one—not altogether western and not altogether eastern. Russia as a political and cultural entity grew up in the Byzantine world. The principality of Kiev, although independent of Byzantine political control, was culturally a Byzantine colony. When Byzantium fell to the Latiņ buccaneers in 1204, and Kiev a generation later to the Mongols, close ties with "Tsargrad" were broken. The center of gravity of the East Slavic world shifted to Muscovy, and for a century and a half nearly the entire East Slavic area was politically controlled by the Golden Horde, itself part of the vast Mongol Empire ruled from Karakorum. The reign of Ivan III (1462-1505) marks a turning point: the so-called "shaking off of the Mongol yoke" was accompanied by a renewed connection with Byzantium when the Tsar of Muscovy married the niece of the last Emperor, and began to regard himself as the heir of the fallen Empire and the only remaining Orthodox monarch. From this period dates the famous doctrine of the "three Romes," formulated by the monk Filofei: "Two Romes have fallen [Rome and Byzantium], the third [Moscow] stands; a fourth there will not be."

Fifteenth century Russian literature belongs entirely to the eastern or Byzantine tradition, and to the medieval world, just as does the Muscovite state. During the height of the western Renaissance, in the lifetimes of Ariosto and Shakespeare and Cervantes and Ronsard, the Russian state and Russian letters are represented by Ivan IV ("the Terrible"), who could solemnly assure the Holy Roman Emperor that he, Ivan, was directly descended from Caesar Augustus, and belonged thus to an older and more legitimate line of emperors than the upstart Hapsburgs!

But even in the sixteenth century there are already some intimations of western influence in the closed world of Muscovy. Ivan's one-time commander and later arch-enemy, Prince Andrei Kurbsky, who abandoned Muscovy for Lithuania-Poland, represents a new world outlook and a new mode of writing. From him to the "westernizers" of the reign of Alexei Mikhailovich the line is direct.

The old royal house of Ryurik died out when the sickly and pious son of Ivan IV breathed his last, at the very end of the sixteenth century. There followed a chaotic and shattering period known in Russian history as the *Smuta*, or "Time of Troubles." Two more or less "legitimate" tsars took the throne (Boris Godunov and Vasily Shuisky), several adventurers pretending to be the dead son of Ivan the Terrible (False-Dimitry I, II, etc) plunged the country into civil war; and the occasion was seized by Muscovy's malevolent neighbors Poland and Sweden to attempt whole or partial annexations. Class conflict was exacerbated: the anarchic Cossacks harried the land, the peasants, driven to desperation by famine and tyranny from their own boyars and foreign interventionists, revolted; and finally a national movement, led by the "middle class" burghers of Nizhny Novgorod ousted the foreigners, put down the revolts, and established a new dynasty of tsars, the house of Romanov. All this lasted for fifteen dreadful years (1598-1613). During this period all the ancient traditions of Rus were shattered, and western ideas, along with Polish and Swedish and other western adventurers, inevitably made their way into Muscovy.

The progress of this "westernization" was accelerated when in 1654 the Ukraine, which had been since the coming of the Mongols a part of the Polish-Lithuanian state, seceded and joined the Tsardom of Muscovy. The union was only partial and led to endless wars between Muscovy and Poland; but the ties thus established were permanent, and a current of western culture began to flow more and more abundantly between the Ukrainian capital of Kiev and backward Moscow.

The new line of the Romanovs is represented in the seventeenth

4

century by Tsar Mikhail Feodorovich (he was the son of Feodor Nikitich Romanov, later Patriarch of Russia under the name of Filaret [1613-1745]), Tsar Alexei Mikhailovich [1645-1676], Tsar Feodor Alexeevich [1676-1682] and two other children of Tsar Alexei, Tsar Peter Alexeevich (Peter I "the Great": 1682-1725) and Tsar Ivan (V) Alexeevich [1682-1696]. Since Peter was a child and his older brother a half-wit, the actual power was held by their sister the regent Sophia until 1689 when her machinations to eliminate her brothers led to her overthrow. The effective reign of Peter the Great can thus be dated from 1689.

It is a widespread misconception shared by Russians and non-Russians alike that modern Russian literature dates from the age of Peter the Great. According to this belief, the program of Russia's great "transformer," to "Europeanize" his backward country, embraced literature as well as government, economics, the calendar, beards, dress, and practically every other aspect of life. The literature which began to be created beginning in the second third of the eighteenth century, and associated with the names of Kantemir, Trediakovsky, Lomonosov and Sumarokov, was, according to this conception, a wholly borrowed item, an exotic plant born in western Europe and acclimatized and naturalized on the uncongenial soil of the Slavic east.

It is doubtful if any such wholesale borrowing has ever in history resulted in a great literature. It is true that Roman literature at first glance appears extraordinarily derivative; yet a close look reveals that in almost no instance has the Greek original been merely copied. Unmistakable Roman elements are everywhere apparent, and it is only because the prehistory of Roman literature goes back into the era of oral, rather than bookish composition, that we have the illusion of a literature created part and parcel by imitation of an older and more advanced model.

The oral stage of Roman literature is lost beyond recall; it never apparently occurred to the Romans to record it, or if they did, such records have disappeared in the course of the ages. The early stages of Russian oral literature have not been entirely lost; folklore songs and ballads (byliny) began to be recorded in the seventeenth century, and this proceeded throughout the next two centuries; to a small extent popular oral literature is still alive even in the twentieth century. It is therefore possible to assess the importance of this factor in the equation in a way that cannot be done with the Roman example; and it becomes clear that, however

5

much Russian literature after Peter may have owed to the West by way of direct borrowing—and it did owe a very great deal—its borrowings did not merely shove the native tradition aside and replace it with an alien strain, as used to be believed, but were in some sense necessitated by native developments which had become ready to assimilate them; and that the true beginnings of the modern period in Russian literature must be dated to a generation at least before Peter's birth. As for the Petrine period itself (1689-1725), far from marking a start, it marks a hiatus. As a brilliant Soviet scholar in the field, Dmitry Likhachev, has well remarked: "In the whole course of Russian history there is no more unliterary period than the era of Peter the Great."[1]

Three currents enter into the stream of seventeenth-century Russian literature: the native medieval tradition, itself a mingling of Byzantine, South Slavic and native folklore elements; the oral or folklore tradition already referred to, which through seventeenth-century recordings becomes a minor object of imitation in writing (the so-called "democratic poetry" of the seventeenth century); and the west European component, which in the seventeenth century came not directly from the foremost European nations, but through Poland and the Ukraine. The elements borrowed from a western European source, however, although belonging to what may be called the "modern literary system" as distinct from the native medieval tradition, are not elements derived from the masterpieces of contemporary west European literatures. Cervantes, Lope de Vega, Corneille, Racine, Shakespeare, Milton—these great names become known and assimilated in Russian culture only a century or two later.

At this point, since we are dealing with very large general questions, it may be well to examine the nature of cultural periodization as it concerns Russia.[2] Going backwards, and leaving the entire moot question of "socialist realism" out of account at this time, we can observe the following well-defined cultural periods, which in each case coincide in time with analogous periods in western Europe: at the end of the nineteenth century and dominating the first two decades of the twentieth (up to World War I and the Russian revolutions) is the somewhat heterogeneous literary and esthetic trend to which no entirely satisfactory name has yet been affixed: "decadence," "symbolism," "modernism," etc. are all used, and all inadequate. It was a movement in part of reaction against "realism," which dominated both in Russia and western Europe from about the middle of the nineteenth century until the 1890s. "Realism" in turn was in part a reaction against "romanticism," to which must be assigned the first half of the nineteenth century and the last two decades of the eighteenth. "Classicism" is identified with most of the eighteenth century. At this point we reach a major question: between "classicism" and the Renaissance in west European cultural history it is now generally agreed to insert the "Baroque" period. But does Russia have a Baroque? Many of the familiar features of the west European Baroque do indeed appear in seventeenth-century Russian poetry: addiction to ornamentation for its own sake, love of extreme contrasts, exaggeration of emotion, particularly of horror, etc. Other features do not appear, however, obviously because Russia's history had taken a different course: there is no trace, for example, of that peculiar religious aspect of the western Baroque which is usually referred to as the "Counter-Reformation." Since Russia had no "Reformation," it also had no "Counter-Reformation." And neither, of course, did it have a Renaissance—which is where the whole substance of its deviation from the western pattern must be placed.

The Renaissance in western European cultural history is a concept so hard to define that some scholars have, in desperation, tried to abandon it, just as they have "romanticism." The concept may be undefinable, but the reality existed nonetheless. The Renaissance was not "caused" by the influx of Greek refugees from the Turkish destruction of Greek Byzantium, as used once to be held; but rediscovery of the classical Greek and Roman "this-worldly" orientation confirmed and strengthened a development already independently going on. Nothing analogous took place in Russia; the medieval "other-worldly" orientation continued to dominate Russia throughout the fourteenth, fifteenth and six-teenth centuries. When glimmers of a break in the medieval tradition can be seen (e.g. Prince Andrei Kurbsky's letters to Ivan IV), it is an exotic and momentary phenomenon without immediate consequence. Eventually, however, something of the liberation of the human spirit from medieval asceticism which the Renaissance brought to western Europe did take place in Russia—but in the seventeenth century! This is why Professor Dmitry Likhachev makes the claim that the Russian Baroque doubled as the Russian Renaissance.[3] However startling this notion may be, it seems to have some solid foundation. Unmistakable elements of Renaissance ideology are certainly detectable in the Russian seventeenth century. Taken as a whole, therefore, this century is a period of bewildering contradiction and complexity.

It is not, however, in Russia a period of great literature. The medieval accomplishment was past—indeed, literature of any kind barely survived the reign of Ivan the Terrible, a period that must be reckoned as a close runner-up of the Petrine era as the "most un-literary age in Russian history." The tradition-shattering events of the *Smuta* contributed still further to the demolition of medieval literary solidity. At the same time the new elements percolating in from the West had not had time to become fully established, and the newly emergent "democratic" literature was still in infancy. The seventeenth century is thus, inevitably, a period of transition, and it has little of permanent literary value to offer. Its literary significance is chiefly that of an age of "forerunners."

Perhaps the most important single mark of the seventeenth century in Russia is one of those belated Renaissance characteristics to which reference has been made—the aggrandizement of the role of personality, as against the medieval subordination of the personal to the collective element. The medieval author was an impersonal embodiment of his group. If we know the names of some chroniclers (Nestor, for instance), we feel their work nonetheless to be only part of a whole the characteristics of which belong not to the person, but the genre. Style in the Middle Ages is never personal, but belongs to the literary type. Whatever their names, most medieval Russian chroniclers sound alike; they follow the same principles of construction, they present the same ideas, they employ the same language. But such seventeenth-century chroniclers as Prince Katyryov-Rostovsky or Avraamy Palitsyn are to a much greater extent individuals, with voices of their own. The text of a medieval work, moreover, is not thought of as an individual, inviolable, fixed entity, into which only its author has the right to make insertions or alterations. Perhaps only the awe accorded such powerful political figures as Vladimir Monomakh or Ivan the Terrible saved their writings from interpolation and addition. But a seventeenth-century text, insofar as it is created under the canons of the modern literary system (e.g., the "Life" of the Archpriest Avvakum or the *virshi* of Simeon Polotsky) is a unique and individual work of art, no more admitting of alteration than, let us say, the text of *Eugene Onegin.* There are various other aspects of the aggrandizement of the role of personality—

the interest in actual, real-life environment rather than an idealized convention, the breakdown in the etiquette of caste portraiture, the emancipation of the imagination in creating plots with purely human motivation, etc.—which we shall discuss in more detail where they can be illustrated by individual works. For the present this may suffice as general characterization of the period.

When in the context of literary criticism we speak of such large-scale cultural periods as "classicism," "romanticism," "Baroque," et al., we imply that the literature created in these periods is patterned upon certain constants which operate in this period and not in the same way in any other. The total picture of the unique and unrepeated characteristics of a literary period we call a "literary system." Such a system will have many distinct parts— use and preference in the matter of genres, use of images and figures of speech generally, conventions of language, etc., as well as a fund of common ideas more or less distinct from those of other literary systems. By way of illustration, the literary system of romanticism contains, among many other distinguishing elements, the following: preference for the elegy, especially in a melancholy and meditative mood, as a primary poetic genre, and for the historical novel as a prose genre; an exaggerated use of metaphor; an attempt to come closer to the speech of everyday life than eighteenth-century classicism approved of; the widespread philosophical concept of what has been called "organicism" (the universe as a living, growing organism, rather than as a machine); the concept of the poet as a prophet, etc. Obviously, of course, no one would maintain the absurd proposition that "melancholy" elegies never existed before the romantic period, or that all romantic elegies are melancholy. But where exceptions to the general picture exist, they are recognizably exceptions, and do not belong to the "literary system" as a whole. There are, of course, no literary absolutes.

The literary system of the Russian seventeenth century is a complicated one, embracing as it does both the not yet extinct genres of the medieval period and the newly created genres which will come to dominate in the modern system. Thus, alongside of such thoroughly medieval types of literature as the encyclopedic compilation ("The Great Mirror," "Deeds of the Romans," "The Brightly Shining Star," etc.) and the saint's life ("Life of Juliania Lazarevskaya," etc.) we find such modern genres as the picaresque novella ("Frol Skobeev") and the first drama ("Comedy of Judith"),

9

etc. A good deal of the writing in the seventeenth century is translation from western originals (not, as has been noted before, from contemporary masterpieces, but from second-rate and old-fashioned works long obsolete on their home ground); thus the three large "collections" mentioned above are seventeenth-century translations respectively of the *Speculum magnum* of Vincent of Beauvais, of the anonymous *Gesta Romanorum*, and of a Belorussian (Catholic) collection of stories about the Virgin, translated into Russian in 1668. The entire popular genre of the chivalric novella is translated, e.g., "Bova Korolevich" (the English "Bevis of Hampton"), "Peter of the Golden Keys," "Basil Golden-Hair," "Apollonius of Tyre," etc.

One of the peculiarities of the literary system of medieval Russia is the total absence of verse.[4] All medieval Russian literature is in prose: even the highly poetical *Song of Igor's Campaign* is, formally at least, in rhythmical prose. This, of course, does not mean that medieval Russia was ignorant of verse; it means that such verse as existed (folk song, *bylina*, etc.) was oral, not written. In any case, it is in the seventeenth century that we encounter for the first time a bookish Russian verse. This peculiar verse system (the syllabic) in its way epitomizes the complication of the seventeenth-century literary picture generally, for into it enter both folklore elements (the so-called *raeshnyi* verse) and foreign borrowings (the Polish system of syllable counting). To this we shall return at the appropriate place.

B. *The Historical Memoir*

Since the writing of verse was, as we have noted, a seventeenth-century innovation, it is natural to begin with a look at the prose genres. One of the oldest of these is undoubtedly the chronicle *(letopiś)*. The origin of Russian chronicle writing certainly goes back to at least the eleventh century, and was stimulated by the example of Byzantine literature, in which the chronicle (e.g. those of John Malalas or of Georgios Hamartolos) was very popular, especially in the less educated circles. The Greek chronicles of Malalas and George "the Sinner" are the basis for the medieval "Chronograph," a kind of world history, put into its final form with the addition of vast amounts of material from later sources by Sergei Kubasov in the seventeenth century. The chronicle as a genre differs of course, from genuine "history" in offering only a year by year account of events, often compiled as they happened, and hence precluded from seeing them as parts of a whole. The chronicle is not necessarily devoid of commentary—the chronicler very often inserts his moral judgment in relating events—but it lacks, by the very nature of its compilation, any possibility of an overall view of the significance of what happens. It will report, year after year, the incursions, let us say, of the barbarian Polovtsy into southern Russia, lament the destruction which they cause and attribute it perhaps to God's wrath for Russia's sins; it may even go far enough to intimate that the internecine quarrels of the Russian princes are the cause of the weakness which makes the nomad raids possible. It will not, however, see the entire picture as a whole, relate the menace of the Polovtsy to that of the Pechenegs who preceded them, or that of the Avars and Huns still earlier. Nor will it see the significance of geographical environment in conditioning different modes of life, settled and nomadic. The nearest the medieval chronicler ever comes to an overall view of events is in the passages where he moralizes over God's grand designs.

The anarchy which filled the first half of the seventeenth century: the extinction of the old royal dynasty, the horrors of usurpation, famine, civil war and foreign intervention both shook the medieval faith in the permanence and solidity of institutions, and stimulated men to record their impressions of what had happened. What was distinctly new about this was the background of the men who did the recording. Medieval chroniclers, from Nestor on, were monks, writing in the relative security of their cloisters, and impersonally and dispassionately recording events which they had witnessed from the outside. But the seventeenth century chroniclers were, or had been, participants. Prince Katyryov-Rostovsky (d. 1640) had been an intimate of Boris Godunov and of the

11

First Pretender; he was exiled by Vasily Shuisky and enjoyed the favor of Mikhail Feodorovich, in whose reign he composed his "Annalistic Book" (1626). The compiler of the anonymous "Other Relation" of 1606, although apparently like Palitsyn, a monk, gives evidence of having been personally involved in the sieges of Moscow and Kaluga, and probably in other events of the "Time of Troubles." The "New Tale of the Illustrious Russian Tsardom and Great State of Muscovy," of 1610, which is oddly couched in the form of an open letter to all Orthodox Russian Christians, is the work, it is conjectured, of a "boyar cadet" (syn boiarsky) or departmental secretary of the capital, with considerable personal knowledge of the events of his time. It may be noted that several of the chronicles of the period, in keeping with medieval tradition, are anonymous; some of them also show signs of interpolation by later hands—another medieval trait. The concept of literary "ownership" of a text has not yet obtained full currency in the seventeenth century.

The most distinguished of the *Smuta* chroniclers is Avraamy Palitsyn. Born about 1555, to an old boyar family, he served in the 1580s as *voevoda* of Kola on the Gulf of Murmansk. In 1588 he suffered disgrace, perhaps in connection with a suspected plot of Vasily Shuisky against Boris Godunov, the all-powerful brother-in-law of Tsar Feodor Ivanovich. He was sent to the Solovetsky Monastery on an island in the White Sea, and forcibly "shorn," that is, made a monk, losing his original name of Averky and assuming the monkish Avraamy (Abraham). After the accession of Boris Godunov as tsar he was recalled to Moscow; and in 1608 Vasily Shuisky, then tsar, appointed him "cellarer" (i.e., business manager) of the very important fortress-monastery of the Holy Trinity of St. Sergius (Troitso-Sergeevsky) north of Moscow. He seems to have exercised his functions *in absentia*, for he was in Moscow during the epic sixteen-month siege of the monastery, which his famous "Relation" describes. After the fall of Vasily Shuisky, Avraamy was sent to treat with the Polish King, then at Smolensk, in the famous "great embassy" of some 300 persons whom the ruling boyars preferred to have out of the capital. He received various favors from King Sigismund, and returned to Moscow in time to help, according to his own account, in the election of Michael Feodorovich as Tsar. When, however, the young Tsar's father, the Patriarch Filaret, returned from Poland in 1619, Avraamy, for reasons obscure to us, was again disgraced and sent to

12

the Solovetsky Monastery once more. It was there that he composed his chronicle of the events of the *Smuta*, and there he died in 1627. Even if we discount his own inflated account of his services in procuring the election of Tsar Michael, it is evident that he had a considerable part in the events which he chronicles. And not only is his chronicle a quite accurate, though tendentious, account of events, but the author makes judgments upon these events that are sometimes independent of the medieval dualism of "good" and "evil." In this respect, as in others, his work lies on the borderline between the medieval and the modern literary systems, and between "chronicle" and "history."

Avraamy Palitsyn's "Relation" *(Skazanie),*[5] or, as the author himself entitled it, "History for the Remembrance of Coming Generations," is evidently put together of diverse materials at various times; it fails altogether in internal unity. The first six chapters constitute what appears like an earlier, independent work, which carries the history from the death of Ivan the Terrible to the overthrow of Tsar Vasily Shuisky (i.e., 1584-1610). Part II of the work (chapters 7-52) is the largest section, and is devoted entirely to the events of the famous sixteen-month siege of the Trinity Monastery of St. Sergius by the Poles. The author, as has been noted, although an official of the monastery, was not present during the siege. He very artistically, however, contrives to give the illusion of an event taking place before the reader's eyes by utilizing day-by-day notes evidently kept by some monk who did go through the siege. He heightens the emotional impact of his account by occasional passages of rhyming prose—a rhetorical device which comes close to, but does not coincide with, some of the earliest forms of Russian verse. One of the most interesting episodes of the siege account is the story of the Polish attempt to mine the wall of the Monastery, and its frustration by the defenders. Part III, entitled "Relation of the Destruction and Liberation of Moscow," carries the story of the *Smuta* from the end of the siege to the expulsion of the Poles from the capital. Part IV relates the election of Michael Feodorovich (1613) and the resumption of ordered government. The short last part (chapters 74-77), which Avraamy entitled "Relation of the Coming from Poland of the King's Son Vladislav Zhigmontov," carries the narrative to the Peace of Deulino in 1618 and to some events of 1620, when work on the whole was evidently broken off, probably by Avraamy's death.

One of the features of medieval historiography which Palitsyn's "Relation" still retains is the evaluation of Russians and Poles from the point of view of the dichotomy "light" and "darkness." The Roman Catholic Poles and their apostate Russian allies are of course "the forces of darkness"; they are referred to as "lions," "wolves," "serpents," etc., while the defenders of the true faith, the "people of light," are figured as "the sheep of Christ the shepherd," etc. It should be noted incidentally that Palitsyn's narrative is altogether silent about his own somewhat questionable relations with the "heretic" Polish King Sigismund. Historical causation also still shows features of the familiar medieval supernaturalism: the valiant monastery is directly watched over by its founder, St. Sergius of Radonezh; the usurpation of the First Pretender (the *Rostriga*) is "prompted by the devil," etc. The narrative, however, has a fervently patriotic intensity which raises it at times to real eloquence; and especially in the first section the author's indignation at the selfishness of the rich and their callousness toward the sufferings of the poor during the famine reaches a prophetic height. These are features which, although not altogether wanting in medieval literature, belong more properly to the modern period. Two short extracts may serve to illustrate the style of Avraamy Palitsyn.

The first of these is taken from the account of the great famine of 1601-03: in the first version, given here, the language is considerably more vigorous than in the later revision.[6]

And on account of these Nikitichi-Iurevye [the father and uncles of the later Tsar Michael, who had been, in Palitsyn's view, unjustly exiled], and because of the witless silence of all the world, which did not dare to speak to the Tsar the truth about the ruin of the innocent, shortly, in the same year 7111 [A.D. 1602-03] the Lord overshadowed the heaven with clouds, and so much rain fell that all mankind fell into fear.

And every agricultural work passed away, and every seed that was sown, after growing up, was beaten down by the innumerable waters that poured from the air; and the wind did not blow upon the grass of the earth for seventy days; and before the sickle was stretched forth a mighty frost smote all the labor of men's works in the fields and in the orchards, and all the earth was as though consumed by fire. And as this year passed and all nature cried out "Oh, oh! Woe, woe!," there was a second year even worse, and likewise even a third. . . .

Even according to the saying of the holy fathers, many at that time turned themselves to the second idolatry [the worship of the "Golden Calf"],

14

and all who had silver and gold and vessels and clothing put them up for sale, and gathered into their houses all the seed of every kind of grain, and received ten-fold profit and more. And in all the cities in all Russia there was a great triumph, with the devil's aid, of the love of money! Many who had money would not incline themselves to divide with their brothers, but beheld on the streets of the sovereign city men dying of hunger, and paid no heed. And there were not so many logs and firewood on carts, as bodies of the naked dead continually being carried throughout the whole city; and for two years and four months, as count was kept at the Tsar's orders, they buried in three common pits 100,027, and even more than this, in the single city of Moscow.

In those years many with wealth said to those who begged from them: We have nothing, in this time of tribulation from all the nations surrounding us, and even more from our own,—and yet innumerable quantities of all sorts of grain were being hoarded, and the long-established granaries were not exhausted, but stood full of sheaves, while the threshing-floors were overflowing with ricks of grain enough for fourteen years, from the beginning of the Confusion in all the Russian land, and they all lived on the labors of years back; for the plowing and sowing and reaping were thrown in confusion, as the sword was always lying at all men's necks. This was, of course, the sin of all Russia, because of which she suffered at the hands of foreign nations; for in the time of the testing by God's wrath, she did not have mercy for her brothers, but locked up her rich granaries for herself and the man-slaying foe [i.e., the devil]. And as we did not show mercy, so shall our enemies not show it to us.

The second extract, from chapter 70 of the "Relation,"[7] describes the feelings of the Russian patriot at the sight of the devastation wrought by the Poles in the Kremlin—the religious center of all Russia:

And with singing of prayers they entered the Kremlin enclosure in a countless multitude of people. And there was in truth a sight deserving of lamentation and pity. For what is madder than this madness, which those accursed savages wrought, together with the thrice-accursed and sacrilegious apostates and informers, the Russian traitors? For they beheld the holy churches of God desecrated and befouled and filled with all sorts of foul vermin [lit., "moths"]. And the holy and revered ikons of the Lord Christ and His most pure Mother in all the sanctuaries cut to pieces and the eyes punched out, and the altars of God defiled and plundered, and every sanctuary laid waste and maliciously plundered, and a multitude of human bodies cut down by those man-eaters, and lying in the sacred vessels. It is not possible to tell all the calamities which those accursed savages wrought, for our sins, in the sovereign city of Moscow. However, according to the Divine

Scriptures, the holy cities of the Orthodox are in no wise defiled, even if they are possessed by the unclean, through God's unfathomable decrees, even as Jerusalem of old. . . . But let us leave these things, for this is not to my purpose. All the army and all the Orthodox people of all ranks entered into the Kremlin enclosure with much joy and gladness, confessing themselves to the Lord. And when the whole consecrated congregation [i.e., the clergy] with a multitude innumerable of people had entered into the great and holy church of the Mother of God, of Her revered and glorious Assumption [i.e., the Uspensky Sobor] , they performed the divine liturgy, and thus departed each to his place, glorifying and blessing the Trinity of God the glorious, to whom be glory forever, Amen.

Avraamy Palitsyn's "Relation" belongs for the most part to the medieval tradition, even though elements of a more modern outlook are apparent in, for example, the strongly marked personal picture of the author, the fairly frequent use of colloquial language, especially in reporting the doings of common soldiers in the defense of the Trinity Monastery, etc. A wholly medieval character, however, belongs to two anonymous chronicles, the so-called "Other Relation" (Inoe Skazanie)[8] and the "Lamentation over the Conquest and Total Destruction of the Exalted and Brightly Shining Muscovite State" (Plach o plenenii i o konechnom razorenii prevysokogo i presvetlogo Moskovskogo Gosudarstva).[9] The first of these owes its peculiar title "Other Relation" to the fact that in many eighteenth-century historical compilations it followed the "Relation" of Palitsyn. It too was written by a monk—probably, like Avraamy, an ex-boyar—of the St. Sergius-Trinity Monastery. It is also sometimes known, from the internal evidence of its dating, as "The Chronicle of 1606." The authors of both works were evidently well acquainted with some of the most popular examples of medieval chronicle writing, e.g. the "Account of the Battle with Mamay" and the "Life of Alexander Nevsky." They were also, unfortunately, acquainted with the pompous, inflated, metaphorical, heavily over-ornamented style of Metropolitan Makarios (1528-63); stylistically the "Other Relation" vacillates between the dry factual account of events and highly emotional and rhetorical outpourings. Medieval genre etiquette is assiduously followed: thus, for example, descriptions of battles are totally lacking in individual character, but are built up of clichés derived ultimately from the Old Slavonic translation of Flavius Josephus's Jewish Wars. The anonymous author of the "Other Relation," with blithe disregard for the truth, enthusiastically

16

attributes all possible, and some highly improbable, crimes to Boris Godunov—among others, self-poisoning (Boris, of course, actually died of a stroke). The world outlook of the author is varied, but entirely medieval: the calamities of the "Time of Troubles" are the visitations of God upon Russia because of the personal sins of her monarchs! Palitsyn at least saw social injustice as the ultimate cause, although he still made divine intervention the immediate instrument of punishment.

Of the two major chronicles of the seventeenth century Palitsyn's is somewhat closer to the Middle Ages, the "Annalistic Book" (*Letopisnaia Kniga*)[10] attributed to Prince Katyryov-Rostovsky is a great deal closer to the modern system. The authorship of this, the most reliable as well as the best written work of its kind, is not altogether certain; the attribution rests on the interpretation of part of the *virshi* with which the author concludes his work:

He who compiles this book
Is the son of the aforementioned Prince Michael, who from Rostov his
origin took;
Because he himself these things in his person saw,
And other things heard from those skilled without flaw;
Whatever he had sought out,
Only this he wrote about.

There seems to be very little doubt that the person who thus modestly introduces himself at the end of his book is Prince Ivan Mikhailovich Katyryov-Rostovsky (d. 1640), an important boyar of the first part of the seventeenth century, a kinsman of the Romanovs, and a one-time intimate of both Boris Godunov and the First Pretender. Under Tsar Vasily Shuisky the prince was relegated to Siberia (as *voevoda*). Since he was resident in Tobolsk after 1608, the last years of the *Smuta* which his work records must have been known to him only through secondary sources— probably from "Those skilled without flaw!"

Prince Katyryov-Rostovsky, unlike Avraamy Palitsyn, was not, as far as we know, in any way closely connected with the church; moreover, he was well read in western literature. The most immediate model for his chronicle was the medieval story of the Trojan War (*Historia destructionis Troiae*) of Guido delle Colonne, a chivalric romance of an entirely secular nature. Prince Katyryov's style, accordingly, marks a sharp break away from the archaistic, over-ornamented, heavily Slavonic prose of Russian writers trained in the monasteries. His work can be rightly regarded as the first appearance of secular prose in modern Russian literature. His sentences are simple, his use of figures of speech is restrained, he avoids as far as possible such long obsolete usages as the Slavonic aorist tense, and his vocabulary is closer to the living language than that of any other literary figure of his century.[11]

The age-old conventional "martial style," deriving from a very early Slavonic translation of Josephus's *Jewish Wars*, reappears in Prince Katyryov's chronicle, but greatly subdued and moderated; note for example this description of the fighting between the armies of Tsar Boris Godunov and the First Pretender, whom Prince Katyryov calls the "Renegade Monk" *(Rostriga)*:[12]

The aforementioned boyars and commanders to Tsar Boris, Prince Feodor Ivanovich Mstislavsky and Prince Dmitry Ivanovich Shuisky with their comrades, came with a numerous army up to the said Novgorod [Seversk] to save it, and they engaged in a very great battle with the Renegade Monk and his army. And the battle was very cruel on both sides, and on this side and on that fell the bodies of the dead; but at the end of the battle, by reason of the sins of Orthodox Christianity, the Muscovite army was defeated, and at once gave itself over to flight. The Poles pursued with the edge of the sword, reddened their hands in the blood of Christians, and wounded severely and threw from his horse the commander of the whole Muscovite army, Prince Feodor Ivanovich Mstislavsky, who was carried wounded from the field of battle. And thus there was a most cruel battle during the day; when at last the sun declined toward the west and the earth was covered with darkness of night, the battle ceased. . . . The captains and commanders, however, of the whole Muscovite army were in no wise frightened of this, and carried out all that had been ordered by Tsar Boris. They set out against the Renegade, and when they had come together in a place called Chemlika, they engaged in a most cruel battle. The rays of the sabres gleamed like the sun, corpses of the dead fell on this side and on that, and thus there was a great battle. The Renegade's army, however, weakened little by little, and gave itself up to flight; but the Muscovite people seized the field and pursued with the edge of the sword; some they killed, some they captured, and some they laid low; and thus were the Poles defeated.

One of the most admired passages of the "Tale from Past Times," and one which marks a stylistic innovation of an almost startling sort is this description of the coming of the spring in 1607; the idyllic picture of nature and the orderly progression of the seasons is artfully juxtaposed with the picture of renewed civil war and the coming of the Second Pretender (the "Ravening Wolf"):[13]

When this winter had passed, and the time had come around when the sun was making his course under the zodiacal circle, and had entered the sign of the Ram, in which sign night becomes equal with day [at the equinox, March 21], and spring is celebrated; the season begins to gladden mortals, gleaming with splendor in the air. As the snow thaws and a mild wind blows and little rills flow into broad streams, then the ploughman digs in with his plough and furrows the sweet glebe, and calls for aid on God the giver of harvest; the grass blades grow and fields grow green, and the trees deck themselves with new leafage; everywhere the fields grow beautiful with fruit, the birds sing their sweet carols—all which peace of every kind, by God's care, according to His love of mankind, comes for man's delectation. In this very time of the fair-faced season the aforesaid ravening wolf made ready with a multitude of warriors of the Polish people and with the Cossacks of the northern country and went forth against the Moscow commanders and against all their army.

The Trojan War narrative of Guido delle Colonne provides its readers with numerous physical descriptions of the principal actors and actresses of his drama. Taking his hint from this source, Prince Katyryov does the same thing with his history. Since he was personally acquainted with many of the monarchs and their families, these descriptions have a liveliness and verisimilitude that are entirely new to Russian narrative literature, where such descriptions have heretofore been mere patchworks of clichés. Of particular interest are the pictures of Ivan the Terrible, the First Pretender, and of the unfortunate daughter of Boris Godunov, Princess Xenia, whose sad fate seems to have particularly moved the chronicler. She was first violated by the Pretender, and then sent to a nunnery:[14]

Tsar Ivan [IV, "The Terrible"] was unbeautiful in figure, with gray eyes and a long and twisted nose; he was very tall in stature, with very high shoulders, a broad chest, and thick arms. He was a man of marvelous intelligence, adequate in bookish learning and exceedingly wordy [see his letters to Prince Kurbsky for confirmation!]. He was bold in battle, and steadfast for his country. To his slaves, who were given to him by God, he was extremely cruel, and he was bold and pitiless as regards the shedding of blood and murder. During his reign he put to death many people, from great to small, despoiled many of his cities, and imprisoned and gave over to pitiless death many of the clergy, and he committed many other acts upon his slaves, and defiled women and girls with fornication. This Tsar Ivan did much good: he loved his army exceedingly, and gave without stint from his treasury what was needed by it. Such was Tsar Ivan.

In this summary it is worth noting that unlike the medieval monk, who passes judgment upon the characters of his chronicle as though in the name of an unerring God, and sees them always as either "good" or "bad," Prince Katyryov portrays the enigmatic Tsar as *both* bad and good, and passes no final judgment upon him. "Such he was," a wholly contradictory figure.

The Renegade Monk [the First False-Dmitry] was of small stature, with a broad chest and thick arms; his countenance did not have the dignity of a tsar, but was coarse-featured, and all his body was extremely dark. He had a keen mind, was most adequate in book knowledge, bold, and extremely loquacious. He loved riding horses; he was a daring fighter against his foes, with valor and might, and he greatly loved the army.

The portrait of the unhappy Xenia is perhaps more conventional, and may owe something to Guido's pictures of Andromache and Polyxena:

The Tsarevna Xenia, daughter of Tsar Boris, for a girl, was a maiden of wonderful intuition, of exceedingly great beauty, extremely white, with red cheeks, scarlet lips, large black eyes, radiant with brightness. When in grief she let fall tears from her eyes, then they were even more radiant with exceeding brightness. Her eyebrows came together, she was faultless in body, suffused with milky whiteness; in stature neither tall nor short. She had black hair, long as a trumpet, and falling upon her shoulders. Among all women she was most pious, and accustomed to book writing, flowering with great excellence of speech, and verily skilled in all her works. She used to love singing voices and was lovingly devoted to spiritual singing.[15]

One of the curiosities of Prince Katyryov-Rostovsky's style is his habit of frequently inserting into the narrative passages of rhythmic prose, often with rhymes at the ends of cola, rhymes which parallel verb forms or noun cases provide in Russian in abundance. These are of course not, as some critics have imagined, a kind of embryonic verse, but a form of ornamentation surprisingly similar in many respects to "Asianic" Greek prose or the peculiar "euphuistic" Latin of Apuleius. At the end of his book

20

the Prince appended a 28-line passage in verse (partly quoted above) of the older sort which it is customary to call by the rather ill-chosen name of "pre-syllabic"—that is, verse with end rhyme in couplets, but with no fixed number of either syllables or accents within each line. The effect of such *virshi* is, to a modern ear, ludicrous; Professor Panchenko rightly remarks[16]: "Syllabic works as a whole can be called verse, but not poetry." The following translation attempts to reproduce as closely as possible this peculiar effect[17]:

A beginning in rhymes,
Of tumultuous times,
Let us with understanding read,
And bid the compiler of this book Godspeed.
This book of annals was compiled
About the coming of a monstrous child [i.e., the First Pretender];
Because he was a beggar in a monkish gown,
And set on his head the imperial crown,
The Tsardom of great Russia harried,
And the imperial diadem on his shoulders carried.
Because this was marvelous in our eyes,
We committed it to writing that forgetfulness might not arise,
And our examples in this book we take,
And to oblivion do not it forsake.
Then there were times of disorder and hurt,
And famous families their fatherland did desert.
We devote our writing to this past event,
And for the admonition of the future generation it is meant.
When on the previous lines we cast our eyes,
The industry of the writer we shall realize.
He who compiles this book
Is the son of the aforementioned Prince Michael, who from Rostov his
origin took;
Because he himself these things in his person saw,
And other things heard from those skilled without flaw;
Whatever he had sought out,
Only this he wrote about.
Let the reader of this to his understanding take,
And things of such importance to forgetfulness not forsake.
This writing to conclusion I have scarcely been able to bring,
And of profit in my labor I have found no thing.

Among the historical and memoiristic works relating to the *Smuta* particular interest attaches to one anonymous "Tale" describing the death of Prince Mikhail Vasilievich Skopin-Shuisky, the mourning for him and his burial.[18] Prince Mikhail, nephew and best general of Tsar Vasily Shuisky, had been sent by his uncle to obtain Swedish help against the Poles and the Second Pretender. Returning from Novgorod with a Swedish mercenary army under the French condottiere Jacques de la Gardie, he defeated the enemy and temporarily relieved Moscow. In April, 1610, however, while at a banquet at the house of I.M. Vorotynsky, for whose son he had been invited to be godfather, he fell suddenly ill, and died two weeks later. Skopin-Shuisky was a popular figure, whose knightly character contrasted sharply with the devious and scheming nature of his uncle, and helped to make the reign of the "boyars' tsar" more palatable. It is not surprising that his sudden death in the flower of his youth (he was 24) should have aroused suspicion of foul play. The "Tale of the Death and Burial" interprets the Prince's demise as the result of poison administered by the malevolent Princess Maria, the child's godmother, daughter of Maliuta Skuratov, who was jealous of Prince Mikhail's fame and popularity. The interesting thing about the *povest'* is the peculiar mixture of styles: at times the narrator follows bookish models of biography—that is, of the "saint's life" genre; and at times he inserts straightforward, factual details of such accuracy that it is evident that he was himself if not an eyewitness, at least a contemporary of the event. But in the description of the crucial scene at the banquet, when Skopin-Shuisky is given the poisoned chalice, and later in his mother's questions when he returns home early and takes to his bed, and in the lamentations by family, friends, and the devoted populace at his funeral, the "Tale" is apparently inspired by a popular ballad on the subject. We have thus an unexampled compilation of the medieval *zhitie* (saint's life), applied in this case to a secular figure, with a folklore (oral) lamentation for a popular hero.

The Middle Ages, in Russia as well as the West, delighted in a literary genre which the modern world scarcely recognizes—the compilation of didactic material, chiefly stories. The huge, amorphous *Chet'ii Minei* of the sixteenth century, put together by the Metropolitan Makarios, contain this kind of material in their conglomerate. The examples from the seventeenth century are mostly translations from western sources, and are no longer exclusively ecclesiastical and "edifying."

The largest of such collections is the "Great Mirror" (*Velikoe Zerkalo*),[19] which appeared in 1677 through the express commission of Tsar Alexei Mikhailovich. The "Great Mirror" is a translation of a Polish translation (*Wielkie Zwierciadło przykładów*) of a fifteenth-century Latin work entitled *Speculum magnum exemplorum*. As the Polish and Latin titles indicate, the content of the "Mirror" is *exempla*—stories with a moral which could be used by preachers to make their sermons more vivid and telling.

The Russian collection contains about 900 stories, less than half of the original number (over 2300), and in other respects too is an adaptation rather than a slavish rendering of the western *Speculum*; this is particularly noticeable in the treatment of stories which have an unmistakably Roman Catholic tinge, which not surprisingly is either toned down or replaced. The Russian of the work is quite bad, with frequent Polonisms. Most of the stories themselves are of a highly moral nature, with a most obtrusive "lesson"; but a few seem, at first sight, to be merely amusing. These, however, the translators are careful to explain, depict conduct which is the result of the Devil's prompting. One such is the short tale entitled: "There is no wrath greater than the wrath of a woman, nor obduracy and intractability more hardened and indomitable":[20]

A husband was going alone with his wife through a cornfield, and said: "This land has been very nicely mowed." His wife in a spirit of contrariness said: "It has not been mowed, but sheared," contradicting her husband greatly. When the husband said: "It has been mowed," the wife said, "sheared." The husband, moved to wrath, threw her into the water. But when in the water she was unable to speak anymore, she held her hand out of the water ,

23

and with her fingers made a sign like a pair of shears, signifying that it had been sheared, and contradicting her husband even to death.

A very popular collection of "moral tales" in western Europe was that known under the title *Gesta Romanorum*. It originated apparently in the thirteenth century, and was an enlargement of an earlier compilation, the *Disciplina clericalis* of Petrus Alfonsi of the eleventh century. The fifteen stories of Petrus's collection were all "exemplary tales," like those of the *Speculum*, intended for the use of preachers. But the larger *Gesta* contains a good deal more of secular material, without obvious didactic value. The name, "Deeds of the Romans," derives from the dominantly classical background of the stories; but these are actually for the most part the kind of "floating tales" which are found everywhere from India to Iceland and can only rarely be traced to an original home.

As with the *Speculum*, the Russian *Rimskie Deianiia*[21] is a partial translation from the Polish, this time a printed edition of 1663 of the *Historiye Rzymskie*. The original Latin text has some 180 tales; both Polish and Russian versions are much shorter, 39 more or less, depending on the manuscript. The stories are told ostensibly for the purpose of moral instruction, but the interest of many of them is centered entirely in the plot, and it is only with a good deal of stretching that a "moral" can be read into them. The translators, however, are at pains to provide such "morals," using, if necessary, an allegorical interpretation. The tales are thus usually followed each by a *vyklad*, or moral exposition. Thus, for example, the tale entitled: "Apologue of the proud emperor Jovian and his fall, and how the Lord God oftentimes opposes the proud but raises up the humble and gives them grace," has a "moral interpretation" which begins as follows:[22]

This emperor can be called every man who is subject to this world, who because of wealth and because of honor is puffed up in his heart unto pride, even as that other king Nebuchadnezzar, who was not obedient unto the admonition of God. He [i.e., Jovian] makes use of such knights, that is, carnal satisfactions, and goes on a hunt, that is, for the vanities of this world; and then a great fever, that is, the Devil's temptation, seizes him, so that he cannot be at rest unless he is cooled in the waters of this world; and this cooling is the killing of the soul, . . .

24

Another popular collection of moral tales is that known in Russian as *Presvetlaia Zvezda*, "The Brightly Shining Star." This was a translation made in 1668 from a Belorussian original. The stories here are all of the type represented in the West by the *Miracula Virginis* (12th century) of Hugues Farsit—that is, stories of the miraculous intervention of the Virgin Mary in human lives. The Catholic origin is betrayed by the excessive reverence for the Virgin, whose cult was more highly developed in the West than in Orthodox countries.

While as the compilations mentioned above amply demonstrate, the "moral tale" was popular, even in the seventeenth century, collections of purely secular stories, some of them quite risqué, also had wide circulation—another indication of the ambivalent position of the seventeenth century, partly medieval and partly modern. A translation dating from 1680 from the Polish, and entitled *Fatsetsii* (i.e., Latin *Facetiae*) contains material going back ultimately to similar collections in Latin, French and German (Poggio Bracciolini, Bebel, Frischlin, Melander et al.). As an example we may cite the story entitled: "On the heaviness of a woman's character":[23]

Some merchants were voyaging by sea from Dantzig to Sweden. By chance there arose a great storm of wind on the sea and the ship was surrounded by waves, and all despaired of their lives. And they began to take thought for their salvation, and gave orders to lighten the ship, by throwing overboard their crates and bales. One certain fellow, not having anything [else] to throw, seized his wife and threw her into the sea. When the mariners began to reproach him for this, he answered: "Neither at home nor on shipboard have I ever acquired anything heavier than this, and for this reason I jettisoned it, along with your burdens."

The ever popular "Fables of Aesop," known in the West throughout the Middle Ages, reached Russia in the seventeenth century, via Poland. Two translations, 1609 and 1675, are known. The 1675 version, entitled: "Spectacle of Human Life" (*Zrelishche zhitiia chelovecheskogo*) is distinguished by its didactic character, the moral becoming the center of the narrative, however loosely it may be connected with the story. After the narrative the translator usually adds references to the authority of classical or medieval writers. A typical example is the fable "Of the tree and the reeds":[24]

Once a tree stood very high, and spread its branches up even to the sky. Greatly exalted by pride, it said: "There is nothing on earth like me." And it mocked the reeds, because they are swayed even by a little wind. And there chanced to be a great wind, and it threw down that tree from its roots. Those reeds, seeing this, all said: "O what a great marvel, that this lofty tree, which used to spread its branches very high and wide, has now fallen and is destroyed, while the little reeds remain unharmed by it."

Thus men who are in great offices are exposed to a fall, while little men stand outside, and if they are shaken by strong winds, they remain unharmed nonetheless.

Such pride did the great city of Tyre display when Alexander the Great, like a mighty wind, came down on the land of Phoenicia. The small cities all submitted to him, and were unharmed by him. But the city of Tyre, trusting in its strength and might, opposed Alexander, and he attacked the city with great force and captured it and killed all the inhabitants and destroyed the houses. Then the little cities said to the purpose: "It behooves one to submit to the stronger." Josephus Flavius writes [the account].

D. The Saint's Life

Next to the chronicle, probably the most prevalent form of prose in the Russian Middle Ages was the saint's life (zhitie). Huge collections of these were made (e.g., the Chet'ii Minei), arranged according to the calendar for pious reading. Translations of Greek Lives were among the earliest compositions in Old Slavonic, and as soon as Russian Christianity began to produce saints of its own, monks turned their hand to writing analogous accounts of their careers. The earliest such Life is that of the princely martyrs Boris and Gleb.

The medieval Vita is a highly conventionalized genre, governed by what Professor Likhachev calls "canons" of appropriate action, and which he picturesquely compares to a kind of "parade uniform" or "full dress" assumed for a solemn occasion. Professor Likhachev's brilliant insight into the psychology of medieval usage can best be conveyed in his own words:[25]

The effort to subordinate the exposition to etiquette, to create literary canons, can also explain the transfer, habitual in the Middle Ages, of descriptions, speeches, formulas, etc., from one work to another. In these transfers there is no conscious effort to deceive the reader, to put forward as historical fact something which in reality has been taken from another literary work. The point is simply that what has been transferred from one literary work to another is first and foremost what was related to etiquette: speeches which *ought* to have been pronounced in a given situation, actions which *ought* to have been performed by the characters under the given circumstances, the author's interpretation of what is going on, appropriate to the occasion, and so forth. What ought to be and what is are intermingled. The writer considers that etiquette determines as a whole the conduct of the ideal hero, and he reproduces this conduct by analogy. . . .

Every reader, in reading a work, takes part as it were in a certain ceremony, includes himself in this ceremony, participates in a certain "action," a peculiar kind of "divine service." The writer of the Middle Ages does not so much portray life, as he transforms it and "decks it out," clothes it in parade, festal costume. The writer is a master of ceremonies. He employs formulas as signs, armorial bearings. He hoists flags, gives parade forms to life, guides the "decencies." Individual impressions are not expected from a literary work. A literary work is calculated not for the individual, separate reader, although the work is read not only aloud for many listeners, but also by separate readers.

Professor Likhachev vehemently insists that "canons" such as he describes are not "clichés." Clichés are worn-out formulas, repeated from one work to another through the sloth or mental poverty of the writer; "literary canons" are the solemn and fitting expression of what a given situation demands ("etiquette"). It would be as unthinkable to abandon these and substitute some novel, individual expression, as it would be to drop the "Our Father" from the liturgy in favor of the priest's own improvised prayer.

"Literary etiquette" such as Professor Likhachev describes begins to break down even as early as the sixteenth century. The breakdown, paradoxically, is accelerated by attempts to make literature even more formulaic; but once new, unprecedented forms are added to the "canons," it is only a step to their complete elimination. The "literary canon" is essentially a generalizing vehicle; it suppresses everything that renders a situation unique, and by giving ritual form to a narrative renders it universal. In a saint's life, for example, certain features are obligatory: the saint must come of a pious and God-fearing family; he must show an early inclination toward good works and an aversion for worldly frivolity; he must practice unusual asceticism; he must be frequently assailed by devils, whom his pious life enrages; during the course of his life he must perform certain miracles, and after his death, his tomb, relics of his body, or even fervent prayer to him must heal the sick, cast out devils, rescue those in peril, etc. If his tomb is opened, the body must be uncorrupted and sweet-smelling. In the composition of a saint's life a practiced church-man will work over the "simple, illiterate" notes which may have been compiled immediately after the saint's death, and if any of these elements is wanting, will add it as a matter of course, while he drops everything which would be local and peculiar to this particular saint. This universalizing and leveling process is particularly noticeable in "Lives" which are to be read in part at services commemorating the saint.

But alongside of the tendency to suppress the concrete and individual traits of a life goes the exactly opposite tendency, to emphasize these characteristics—what Professor Likhachev calls a "realistic tendency." This realistic tendency begins to show up as early as the sixteenth century, and is quite prominent by the seventeenth. Two examples of this may be cited, one an individual "saint's life" composed by a layman, the other a whole sub-genre of lives of the saints from the far northern region of Russia, particularly those connected with the great Solovetsky Monastery on an island in the White Sea. In this region, for some reason, the concrete details of the hard lives of fishermen and mariners came to dominate the entire structure of the composition.

"The Life of St. Juliania Lazarevskaya" (d. 1604)[26] was written, about ten years after her death, by her son, Kallistrat Druzhina-Ozorin, a boyar from the province of Murom. There may be some significance in the place of his origin, since one of the most notable "Lives" of the sixteenth century, that of "Peter and Fevronia," which is a vivid retelling of two well-known folk tales, is localized in Murom. It is a sober and factual account in a style quite at variance with the exuberant rhetoric that dominates the sixteenth century.

The "Life of St. Julania" is not, in form, a radical departure from the "saint's life canon": Julania comes of a pious and God-fearing family; she irritates the relatives who bring her up after her parents' death by her ascetic practices and aversion to games; she is beset by devils, but routs them with the aid of St. Nicholas; she resorts to extreme mortification of the flesh in her old age, sleeping on rough pieces of firewood and putting broken nutshells and potsherds into her shoes. A miraculous voice is heard by the local priest, declaring her a saint; after her death, her body is found uncorrupted and her coffin is full of sweet-scented myrrh which cures the sick, etc. What represents a really radical innovation, however, is the nature of Julania's life apart from these conventionalities. She rarely has the opportunity of even going to church, since she lives most of her life on country estates; she is married and raises a numerous family (thirteen!); her husband refuses her request, after a serf has killed her eldest son, to retire to a convent, although he agrees to live with her thenceforth "without carnal intercourse"; along with her austerities her son enumerates her household industry: she and her maids work late at night making embroidery which she sells and gives the proceeds to the poor. She is a careful and scrupulous manager of her large estate during the frequent and sometimes protracted absences of her husband on government service; she is kind and helpful to her serfs, she deprives herself of food during times of famine to feed the poor, etc. All this is told in a quiet, unpretentious but dignified style by a layman, with none of the rhetorical flourishes that characterize most such works. The author, moreover, is the saint's own son, and his picture is a warm, sympathetic portrait of a woman whom he himself has known and loved, and the homely details of whose life he enjoys giving. It is noticeable to what an extent the miraculous element is played down. Julania's sainthood is not attested so much by spectacular miracles as by a life of compassionate devotion to the welfare of others.

The "Life of St. Julania" is not entirely a unique specimen; something of the same sort may be found in the anonymous "Life of the Boyarina Morozova, Princess Urusova, and Maria Danilova,"[27] three saintly martyrs of the "Old Ritualists" who died in prison for their beliefs in the reign of Alexei Mikhailovich. But the most remarkable and consistent breach of the literary canons of saints' lives is to be sought in the highly interesting stories of the lives of the saints from the White Sea region.

There are several groups of these "northern lives," most of which have not been published, but remain in manuscript collections of the great Russian libraries of Moscow and Leningrad. Many of the individual "Lives" come from the last years of the sixteenth century, and are thus older than the "Life of St. Juliania." They are remarkable for several things: their language, which although mostly the conventional Church Slavonic, often includes words and expressions from local dialects; their vivid, often first-person narratives of the miraculous interventions of the saints, narratives which tend to become simply exciting stories of harrowing adventure, in which the ecclesiastical and miraculous element plays a quite minor part; and the natural, convincing psychology of the actors in them. Two examples are good enough in themselves to be quoted; they illustrate perfectly all the peculiarities of the type, and demonstrate to the fullest the degree to which the seventeenth century, or in this case even the sixteenth, even when employing the entirely medieval hagiographic genre, has succeeded in transforming it.

The two stories which follow are part of the report of the miracles performed by the sainted founders of the Solovetsky Monastery on the island of Solovky in the Gulf of Onega, an arm of the White Sea. St. Savvaty was one of the original founders of the Monastery in 1429; the first church was built by St. Zosima in 1436. The island, which is one of several in Onezhsky Zaliv, is located at 65 degrees north latitude, and is therefore very cold, although the climate is somewhat moderated by the northern end of the Gulf Stream.

Both stories are quoted, in part or in full, in the very interesting chapter by L.A. Dmitriev, "The Genre of North Russian Saints' Lives," in the Volume: *History of the Genres in Russian Literature of the Tenth to Seventeenth Centuries.*[28] Professor Dmitriev summarizes portions of the first tale, which will be quoted using his epitome:

Among the miracles recorded in the first quarter of the sixteenth century (between 1514 and 1529) by Abbot Vassian, three miracles are the stories of a certain elder [*starets*] Savvaty. They are all, in one way or another, connected with the theme of seafaring, are distinguished by liveliness of exposition, and by their plot-oriented character. The first of Savvaty's stories is the tale "Of the two men who were suffering on Shuzhmuy Island." Here is what the elder Savvaty related to Vassian. This event occurred when Isaiia was abbot. Not long before Easter Isaiia, coming out of his cell in great perturbation, suddenly turned to the brothers with these words: "Who of you, brothers, is willing to take the trouble to go to the island of Shuzhmuy?" (This island is located 60 versts from the Monastery [to the south. W.E.B.].) The narrator continues: "We questioned about the matter: 'On what account, father, are you sorrowful and enjoin such an unexpected and dangerous service?' For the sea was not cleared of ice, which lay very thick, and everything simply forbade such an undertaking." The abbot says that on Shuzhmuy "Orthodox Christians are suffering in great misery." "My heart," continues Savvaty, "was wounded at the abbot's mission, but I told nobody of this, but the desire came to me not to disobey the abbot." After a certain time the abbot sent Savvaty with another monk on monastery business to Virma (a monastery village on the river of the same name near the White Sea). After reporting a heavenly sign repeatedly seen by him before sailing from Solovky, which reminded him "of the abbot's commission," Savvaty goes on with the story: " . . . We began to sail on the sea. With a favoring wind, we landed on a certain skerry [luda, a local name for a small rocky islet], a place called Gab-luda, about 15 versts from Shuzhmuy Island. And there we stopped." Savvaty and his companion Ferapont spent the night on Gab-luda and "We kindled ourselves a fire on account of the wintry cold, as soon as it was night. I lay down with my shoulders to the fire, not sleeping, only warming myself, while brother Ferapont slept in the boat." Here Savvaty had a vision of a certain man who asked him whether he was going to Shuzhmuy. Savvaty answered that he was, if God ordered and Saints Savvaty and Zosima gave their blessing. Then the mysterious stranger said: "God blesses you, go," and disappeared. On the next day Savvaty and Ferapont arrive safely in Virma and carry out their business. Savvaty "began to question those who lived there if there were any people wintering on Shuzhmuy Island. And they informed me: 'A boat,' they said, 'was wrecked there at the very start of winter.' " On the return trip, despite his companion's objections, Savvaty makes a visit to Shuzhmuy Island. "We began to walk over the island with great difficulty, the snow being very deep. . . . And then we found in a certain spot among the rocks a small hut, and in it two men naked and famished, and their feet very frostbitten, and scarcely alive. And when they saw us, they suddenly began to shout as loud as they could." These men relate to their rescuers that while they were wintering on the island two monks had come to them, who called themselves Savvaty and Zosima, and helped them endure all the hardships of wintering; that they had just been there, immediately before their arrival, and had said that rescuers would speedily come for them. When they sailed away from Shuzhmuy, the boat began to be bound in ice. "And the brother, Ferapont, who was with me, began to reproach me for picking up the sick ones." But behold, a passage was made through the ice, and the seafarers reached the monastery safely.[29]

The second narrative, again vividly told in the first person by the man involved, a certain Andrei, comes from the mid-sixteenth century. The story is quoted in full by Dmitriev:[30]

In the year 7046 (1538). On the shore of the ocean sea, on which is the settlement of the saints [i.e., Savvaty and Zosima], that is, Solovetsky Island, many of the inhabitants along the many rivers have the habit of panning salt. A certain salt-panner had occasion to take his salt-pan [*tsren*, a local word] from the salt-works to his home, and he sent after it his hired man named Andrei. "I put the *tsren* on the water," said Andrei, "and was minded to take it on the sea along the shore to the place where I had been ordered. It was a distance of about ten versts to that place. So I stood on the *tsren* and began little by little to move myself forward. On the holes of the *tsren* I put sods. And I came as far as a place where there were a great many rocks, and I wanted to go around those rocks. And suddenly a fierce wind from off shore began to blow. I was frightened, and the water began to rise, and I began to sail in the *tsren* on the deep sea. And the waves rose and great billows, and in the twinkling of an eye I had floated so far away that I could not see the shore, not even the high mountains that stand along the seacoast. And I, poor wretch, began to sob and weep in despair for my life. And I bethought me how, on such waves, like mighty mountains, my leaky *tsren* was sailing. And after this I had an idea, since all of us who live along the seacoast have the habit, in all our misfortunes on sea or land, of calling for help on the wonder-working saints of Solovky. And I began to pray, saying: 'O great wonder-working saints Zosima and Savvaty, show mercy and save me from dreadful death!' So I pray, and make vows for my sins in utter despair, and do not even believe that I am alive. And I am carried for two days and two nights over the deep sea. And I was exhausted, neither eating nor drinking nor sleeping. And from great weariness and hardship I hardly breathed. And again, bitterly sighing, I said: 'O holy wonder-workers Zosima and Savvaty! Either save me, or quickly drown me. Do this quickly!' Then suddenly it seemed to me that from the saints' monastery appeared a black and terrible cloud. And the sea began to toss from the wind of that cloud even more than from the first waves. And I spoke reproachfully and said: 'O holy wonder-workers, in vain did I call on you—you have given me no help.' And there was at that time a great rain, and black darkness on the sea. And I stood neither alive nor dead. The sod on the holes had washed away, and I put the sleeve of my coat down and stood on it. And I was already too weak to stand, or even sit, but I fell on the *tsren* like a dead man, and lost consciousness. I was neither asleep nor awake, only I saw someone in the form of my father saying to me: 'You have been ordered to haul up this *tsren* on land.' And I awoke and saw the shore standing close to me, and I recovered strength and began to rejoice. And from my joy I could not see what to do. And suddenly my *tsren* grounded. I stood on my feet up to my neck in water, and I got out on to shore, thanking Almighty God and His saints, the holy wonder-workers Zosima and Savvaty. I recognized the place where I had come ashore: just where I had been ordered to put the *tsren*, there it had grounded. And when the water went down, according to its custom [i.e., at ebb tide], I found my *tsren* standing on a flat rock. And then he who had sent me saw me, rejoiced greatly and pulled up his *tsren*. But I went to the abode of the saints to work in the monastery to the end of my life, to the glory of Christ our God and to the memory of His saints, the reverend fathers Zosima and Savvaty, the chiefs of Solovky."

Гисториа охрабромъ и ославномъ витезе Бове
Королевиче и осмерти отъца его

Внекоторомъ царствие и велиномъ граде въ славномъ
Граде Антоне силъ Король имене Гандонъ иꙁнялъ онъ града
Дементиана инороя ниꙗрита Зерзауровича доче припрекную
пороленну ꙗнднтрику непреде Гандона схватилса Король имене
дадонъ инороленна спрохелани делание заꙁадена взатустно
ꙗꙁесꙗ ноотцъ ея несовлаговалъ жнила пороленна мнлитриса при
Тода хнеловꙗ свтпдено продила хравшего витеꙁа бову породе
днча нетоари уꙁпищенне полесъ свꙗего раба ссꙗмотой унерпло
дндону чтовъ понꙗ споннество прнехъ плуса свꙗувилъ нове
щꙗеꙗ пвелукнꙗ нꙗ любꙗ сꙗпти свдꙗдено ицпоре дедо прнехъ
иста ппрелно песте инороленꙗ пришедшн пѣнꙗ напрꙗ дꙗ спасꙗну
спрошенне тонꙗ ѣ спꙗꙁꙗн увѣꙗго оруну тоꙗею днꙗꙁꙗ ꙁꙁпрꙗ
днти пнеалꙗ сꙗпопꙗ нꙗчи наꙗпꙗдꙗꙁꙗ сꙗꙗ пенꙗпꙗ повꙗ онеꙗе скоро то
плꙗ прнꙗ ꙁнꙗпꙗрꙗтꙗ средꙗнꙗ иꙗпꙗла дндонъ увꙗ Гандонꙗ

Ипотедицꙗ раꙁости перелꙗ ꙁенꙁꙗꙗ андроꙗꙁꙗ спꙗречнꙗꙗ ꙁꙗпемꙗ
короꙗемъ марнабруномъ ꙁꙗꙁꙗꙁꙗ сохꙗꙗꙁꙗ сꙗꙗ бова пороꙗꙁꙗꙁꙗ спꙗꙁꙗ де
пнꙗꙗ днꙗ иꙗꙗꙁꙗ иꙗꙗꙁꙗꙁꙗꙁꙗ сꙗꙗꙁꙗ марꙗꙁꙗꙗ поꙗꙁꙗꙗꙗꙁ
ꙗꙁꙗꙁꙗ пꙗꙗꙁꙗꙁꙗ прꙗꙁꙗꙁꙗꙁꙗꙁꙗ цꙗꙁꙗ пꙗꙁꙗꙁꙗ сꙗꙁꙗꙁꙗꙗꙁꙗ иꙗ
ꙗꙁꙗ пꙗꙁꙗ пꙗꙁꙗ цꙗꙁꙗꙁꙗꙁꙗ поꙁꙗ сꙗꙗ ꙗꙁꙗ пꙗꙁꙗꙁꙗ пꙗꙁꙗꙁꙗ
бꙗ ꙗꙁꙗꙁꙗꙁꙗ тꙗꙁꙗ доꙗꙁꙗ неꙗꙁꙗ ноꙗꙁꙗꙁꙗꙗ ноꙗ бова ноꙗꙁꙗ
ꙗꙁꙗꙗ пꙗꙁꙗꙁꙗ пꙗꙁꙗ ꙗꙁꙗ оꙗꙁꙗ тꙗꙁꙗ боꙗꙁꙗ пꙗꙗ сꙗꙁꙗ прꙗ
ꙗꙁꙗ ноꙁꙗ пꙗꙁꙗꙁꙗ ноꙁꙗꙗ бꙗ ꙗꙁꙗ пꙗꙁꙗ пꙗꙁꙗ поꙗꙁꙗ сꙗꙁꙗ
чꙗꙁꙗ прꙗꙁꙗ ноꙗꙁꙗ ꙗꙁꙗꙗ чꙗꙁꙗ ꙗꙁꙗꙗꙁꙗ ꙗꙁꙗꙁꙗ
ꙗꙁꙗ уꙗꙁꙗꙗ пꙗꙁꙗꙁꙗ бова пꙗꙁꙗ поꙗꙁꙗ поꙗꙁꙗ ꙗꙁꙗ пꙗꙁꙗ
чꙗꙁꙗ сꙗ пꙗꙁꙗ ноꙗꙁꙗ поꙗꙁꙗ уꙗꙁꙗ бꙗꙗꙁꙗ пꙗꙁꙗ поꙗꙁꙗ
ꙗꙁꙗꙁꙗ сꙗꙗꙁꙗ боꙗꙁꙗ уꙗꙁꙗ ꙗꙁꙗ ноꙗꙁꙗ ꙗꙁꙗꙁꙗ ꙁꙗ ноꙗꙁꙗ
поꙗꙁꙗ боꙗ пꙗꙁꙗ ноꙗꙁꙗꙗ ꙗꙁꙗ ноꙗꙁꙗꙗ ноꙗꙁꙗ бꙗ
пꙗꙁꙗ ноꙗꙁꙗ пꙗꙁꙗ прꙗꙁꙗ ноꙗꙁꙗ поꙗ уꙗꙁꙗ пꙗꙁꙗ ноꙗ
пꙗꙁꙗ поꙗꙁꙗꙗꙁꙗ пꙗꙁꙗ ноꙗꙁꙗ пꙗꙁꙗ поꙗꙁꙗ уꙗꙁꙗꙗ

The popular print ("lubok") of the 17th and 18th centuries often had risque themes in the spirit of the rascal tales such as "Frol Skobeev." In this one three young women make an obscene suggestion for growing hair on the bald old man, but his own ribald gesture outdoes theirs.

Title page of a copy of the "Life of St. Alexei, Metropolitan of Moscow," early 17th century.

CHAPTER II

PROSE GENRES OF MODERN TYPE IN SEVENTEENTH CENTURY RUSSIAN LITERATURE

A. Differentiation in Seventeenth Century Russian Literature

The chronicle, the compilation of instructive material, the saint's life—these were the most important of the medieval genres which survived into the seventeenth century, and which indeed can be found vestigially even in the eighteenth. None of them, as we have seen, maintained in the seventeenth century its medieval character quite unchanged: the individual, personal element intrudes noticeably into both the chronicle and the saint's life, and the "instructive" material which forms the substance of the compilation more and more frequently assumes the purpose of pure entertainment. But medieval genres in the seventeenth century account for only a part of the total literary output; new literary types appear, partly through borrowing, and partly through the appropriation of sub-literary forms.

As Professor Likhachev has acutely observed, medieval literature, art, philosophy, music, etc., are "all of a piece." Their characteristics are those of what he calls a "period style"—the Romanesque or the Gothic. Literature is divided horizontally into a large number of distinct genres, each with stylistic characteristics of its own, which almost, if not quite, exclude the appearance of individual distinctions of style. But there is no vertical division: a chronicler may be a prince or a monk or a bishop, an old man or a youth—his style will be that of the genre, and not of his social position. With the seventeenth century this changes. For the first time in this century a social differentiation makes its appearance:

a distinctive "court literature" is evolved, in conjunction with the increasingly centralized monarchy of the Romanovs; and the oral or "folklore" literature of the illiterate common people is reduced to writing for the first time, and imitations or adaptations of it are created. Both these developments concern chiefly literature in verse, which as has already been noted, appears for the first time in Russian literature in this century. We shall leave consideration of this part of the complex picture of seventeenth-century Russian literature until we have finished a review of the prose.

B. The "Baroque" Period in Russian and Western Literatures

Before turning to the fairly extensive seventeenth-century Russian literature of modern type, we may as well pause briefly to consider the relation of this literature to the contemporary litteratures of western Europe. It is customary at present, and has been for some two or three decades, to distinguish a "Baroque period" in literature, as well as in art, architecture and music, between the Renaissance and eighteenth-century classicism. Some of the characteristic features of literary Baroque can best be illustrated from one of its most typical representatives, Calderón de la Barca. It revels in exaggeration and hyperbole; passions are screwed to the highest pitch, and expressed in ornate, striking, often grotesque images. Contrast, of the most violent sort, is made a central feature of both structure and style—e.g. Calderón's drama *Devotion to the Cross*, with its juxtaposition of murder, lust and perfervid religious mysticism. This principle of contrast is often philosophically treated as a "harmony of opposites"—*discordia concors*. In the figurative arts emotion is expressed in contorted and unharmonious attitudes—e.g. Bernini's St. Teresa, or in

38

unnaturally colored or dimensioned natural scenes or human actors, e.g. El Greco's landscape of Toledo or "St. Martin and the Beggar." In literature there appears a tendency toward the extravagant use of mythological ornamentation and a preference for elaborate, stylized, highly intellectualized figures of speech—e.g. Góngora's *Soledades* or Donne's poems. Characteristic of much baroque prose is the kind of extreme stylization and artificiality known in English under the title "euphuism," in France under that of "préciosité," etc.

Russia, as has often been noted, bypassed the Renaissance. Professor Likhachev distinguishes, in the fourteenth and fifteenth centuries, a "Pre-Renaissance," which other scholars are rather reluctant to accept; but even he admits that the Renaissance itself, which he characterizes chiefly as the liberation of all aspects of culture from religious and "otherworldly" domination, never appears in Russia. In his view, however, a culture cannot thus bypass an important stage of development without in some later stage "catching up" what has been missed.[1] In Russia this process of compensatory "catching up" took place, according to Likhachev, in the seventeenth century, and accounts for some characteristics of the Russian Baroque which set it markedly apart from its western counterpart. It is much less extreme in all its manifestations; instead of terrifying violence and overwhelming contrasts, it exhibits calm and harmony. In art, bright and cheerful colors predominate, painful scenes are avoided or softened, and in general much of the classical sunniness and humanism of the Renaissance appears thus belatedly in the seventeenth century. These qualities, incidentally, make it sometimes difficult to determine the exact line of demarcation in the eighteenth century between the "baroque" and classical periods. For example, do Trediakovsky and Lomonosov belong to the first or the second of these periods? They exhibit characteristics which would make either classification plausible. While too much should certainly not be made of Professor Likhachev's observations, and they should least of all be used as a foundation for establishing a rigid "pattern" in literary history (which he does not do), they do without question have a certain validity and can be used with circumspection in dealing with the Russian Baroque. It should be noted also that in Russia the baroque style, in both the figurative arts and in literature, is pretty much confined to the court literature and art.

To refer once more to Professor Likhachev's very stimulating and often controversial literary theories,[2] he makes a certainly valid distinction between what he calls a "period style" or a "trend" or "direction" (napravlenie). The "period style" is all-pervasive: it affects the entire range of cultural activity. The "trend" or "direction" is restricted to a few, or even to one, area. In his overall view of the course of European culture since the end of the antique civilization, Likhachev distinguishes alternate *primary* and *secondary* styles, the distinction being founded ultimately on phases of economic and social evolution. Primary styles are: the Romanesque, the Renaissance, the Classical, and the Realistic. Between these he inserts, as secondary styles, the Gothic, the Baroque, and the Romantic. By implication, although he never explicitly admits that Realism, to which he gives an exceptional and all-encompassing position, can be followed by anything else, "Decadence," "Symbolism," or "Modernism," or whatever other label may be attached to post-realist cultural achievement, would be another "secondary" style, and as such restricted. The secondary styles, in his view, are more formalistic, less rooted in national character, and hence more readily exportable. This accounts for the wide diffusion of the "Baroque" style throughout Europe, from its original cradles in Italy and Spain. In the succession of styles, whether primary or secondary, he notes the characteristic narrowing of the cultural area which the given style affects: as differentiation progresses among the various arts and sciences, the all-pervading "period style" becomes more and more restricted until it becomes merely a "literary trend," with few if any corresponding features in other cultural manifestations outside of literature. Thus, the Baroque "embraces not only architecture, but esthetic norms harmonize with it in the representative and applied arts, in the art of words, in music . . . [but] I think that the Baroque does not take in science; less definitely than the Romanesque style it is expressed in political thought and daily life." "Classicism takes in only architecture, the representative arts, music, the applied arts, the art of gardens and parks." "Romanticism is still narrower. Architecture is only weakly subordinated to it, although it is powerful in literature, music, painting, the ballet." When we come finally to realism (and Likhachev denies the unscientific application of the term "realistic" to any cultural manifestation outside of the nineteenth and twentieth centuries), he narrows the concept still further: "Realism is a style of literature (and of prose predominantly) and of the representative arts, but it is already less clearly apparent in music, and the ballet does not harmonize with it. It is impossible in architecture. Beyond this go only trends in literature, painting, and architecture."

C. The Exemplary Tale: "Savva Grudtsyn"

With these preliminary generalizations out of the way, we may turn to a consideration of the prose genres of modern type which the seventeenth century has to show. There is a considerable number of these, with origins which are often very complex: influences from the west, usually by way of Belorussian or Ukrainian intermediaries, are important here; and elements evidently connected with the oral literature of the common people crop up in the written literature, especially in such a genre as the parody or the prose satire. There even seems to be a recrudescence of the prose "romance" of Hellenistic times, probably by way of Byzantium, although this "influence" may not have been direct, but again mediated by the west.

Something very closely akin to the Spanish *picaresca* makes its appearance, with antecedents that are not quite clear; and again, whether with direct or oblique western influence, the autobiography (of Protopop Avvakum and other "Old Ritualists") appears for the first time in Russian literature since the medieval period (the "Testament" of Vladimir Monomakh).

Prose literature of modern type in the seventeenth century falls in general into the category of narrative, with a considerable number of different genres. Let us begin with one which still retains medieval connections, the "exemplary tale." The best

41

representative of this is "The Tale of Savva Grudtsyn."[3]

It is significant that the background of this "Faust" tale is the "Time of Troubles," when Russian life and traditional modes of thought were so shattered by anarchy, famine, civil war and foreign intervention, that they were never again to recover. Savva Grudtsyn is the son of a well-to-do merchant family of north Russia. In undertaking a business trip for his father he stops in Orel and looks up one of his father's old friends, Bazhen Vtory. Vtory's young and oversexed wife seduces him. The "Tale" attributes this conduct, in medieval fashion, to a supernatural force: "The Devil, that enemy who hates all things not vile in the human kind, having seen the young man's virtuous way of life, decided to bring strife into the house by inducing Bazhen's wife to have sinful relations with the young man." Savva, however, after a lengthy series of sins with the woman, culminating in one act on the most holy Ascension Day, repents and leaves Vtory's house. He is, however, tormented by desire for Bazhen's wife, and on one occasion, while walking in the fields, has the terrible thought: "If someone, man or devil, would do something so that I might take sexual pleasure with this woman, I would serve even the Devil." This unuttered thought is enough; the Devil comes at once, in the form of another young man (actually a kind of evil double of Savva himself—the personification of his rebellious, sensual self). With the Devil's aid, Savva is able again to resume relations with Bazhen's wife, but not before he has been induced, in the traditional way, to sign away his soul. An interesting episode takes up most of the central part of the "Tale," as Savva, with the Devil's assistance, becomes a captain of mercenaries in the Tsar's service against the Poles. Finally, as the young man begins to be restive under the demon's power, the latter torments him physically until his life is despaired of. The sympathetic Tsar, in gratitude for Savva's services, has him carried to the Church of the Holy Virgin of Kazan, and when the Devil again begins to torment him, Savva cries out: "Help me, my Lady and Holy Virgin!" Help is immediately forthcoming, and the Virgin returns to the erring youth the written contract which he had made with the Devil (it falls from the cupola of the church!), completely erased. Savva, of course, gives all his wealth to the poor and retires to end his days in a monastery.

The "Tale" has numerous interesting and significant facets. In the first place, it is evidently intended as a moral and warning example to the reader of the perils of departing from the traditional medieval code of conduct. Rebellious individualism is a certain road to hell, unless there is genuine repentance. On the other hand, however, while the "exemplary" aspect of the story is certainly the most prominent, there can be no doubt that the military episode, which introduces actual characters, such as General Shein, from the Time of Troubles, and is thus a kind of rudimentary "historical novel," is a concession to the new taste of the time for purely entertainment literature. As to the substance of the central plot, it derives, by what channels we do not know, from a medieval Greek original from which in a very devious way, the legend of Dr. Faustus may also derive. The prominence given in the "Tale" to the intervention of the Virgin points to Polish or Belorussian, i.e., Roman Catholic, influence. The style of the "Tale" is awkward and unliterary, a curious hodgepodge of the colloquial and the bookish.

D. The Historical Romance: "Tale of the Founding of the Page's Monastery"

Several of the anonymous seventeenth-century Russian narratives have an—at least ostensible— historical basis, although this, as with "Savva Grudtsyn," is part of the background and does not constitute the principal matter. One of the finest of these narratives, which combines religious with secular themes, is the "Tale of the Founding of the Page's Monastery of Tver."[4] The "Tale" begins: "In the year of the world's creation 6773 [i.e., A.D. 1265] the Page's Monastery was founded, through the care and solicitude of Great Prince Yaroslav Yaroslavych of Tver [Yaroslav II, brother of Alexander Nevsky: Grand Duke of Vladimir 1263-76] and his

wife, the Great Princess the pious Xenia, in the fourth year after
their union in lawful marriage, and at the request and entreaty of
his beloved page Grigory, Gury in his status as a monk." This sets
the stage for the lengthy account, which is filled with folklore
elements, of the romantic union of the Great Prince with the
beautiful Xenia, a sexton's daughter. The page Grigory was a very
great favorite of the Great Prince, who sent him on one occasion
to collect taxes from the village of Edimonovo. Here he put up
at the house of the sexton, and fell in love with the latter's exceedingly beautiful daughter Xenia. Grigory asked at once for the
girl's hand, and met with no opposition from the father. When,
however, he requested the Prince's permission, the latter tried to
dissuade him on grounds of inequality: as a nobleman Grigory
should not marry a commoner. Grigory, however, was insistent
and the Prince gave in at last, and the page returned to Edimonovo
to make arrangements for the wedding. That night the Prince
dreamed that while hunting his favorite falcon brought him a
dove "of a beauty more exceeding bright than gold." In the morning therefore he set out on a hunt with his falcons. His favorite
falcon refused to return to his hand, and led him, without his
realizing it, to the village of Edimonovo, where it perched on the
church steeple. Meanwhile Xenia, a "wise maiden," i.e., endowed
with second sight, has told her father that Grigory will not be her
husband—he is only the matchmaker (svat). When the Great
Prince, in pursuit of his falcon, appears unheralded, Xenia proclaims who he is, and that he is her bridegroom. And indeed at
sight of the girl's beauty, Prince Yaroslav does immediately claim
her as his own, and bid his beloved page look for another bride.
Grigory departs hearbroken, goes into the forest, and near where
the river Tvertsa falls into the Volga, he founds an oratory. He is
discovered at last and reunited with his Prince, but the Virgin
has meanwhile appeared to him in a dream and commanded him
to found a church and a monastery near the site of his forest retreat. Prince Yaroslav, at Grigory's entreaty, builds the monastery,
and Grigory becomes a monk there, under the name of Gury, and
soon dies and is buried there.

From this synopsis it is easy to see the folklore influence on
the story. The prophetic dreams, Yaroslav's for instance, with the
well-known symbolism of the beautiful dove as a maiden, and of
the favorite falcon as a favorite page; the motif of the falcon leading

44

its master to the girl who is to be his bride; and especially the presence of the "wise maiden"—all this can be paralleled in folk stories in both prose and verse. Quite notable in the development of the plot is the absence of the usual medieval source of conflict —an evil principle battling with the good. Grigory and his master are devoted friends; their both loving the same girl is an unfortunate trick of fate, but neither of them is at fault. The Prince is depicted as simply fulfilling his inevitable destiny when he displaces his friend as Xenia's bridegroom. And the girl's conduct is represented as dictated by her second sight, her knowledge of "what is to be," against which there can be no rebelling. She is not "unfaithful" to Grigory, because she has never recognized him as her bridegroom—he is only the matchmaker. It is worth noting, too, that Xenia's knowledge of the future, while supernatural in a sense, is in no way linked with religion: no saints or angels appear to warn her. The only divine intervention is the vision of the Virgin to Grigory, bidding him build a church. The tale is among the best evidences of the interpenetration, which begins in the seventeenth century, of the genuinely popular, or folklore, element into literary composition. And the "Tale of the Founding of the Page's Monastery" is literary: the language is correct and literate Russo-Slavonic, with none of the gross grammatical errors and oversights of such a vulgar piece as the "Tale of Bova Korolevich" or the "Tale of Eruslan Lazarevich," which we have next to consider.

E. *The Chivalric Romance: "Bova Korolevich" and "Eruslan Lazarevich"*

The "Tale of the Founding of the Page's Monastery of Tver" appeals to a modern reader as a charmingly romantic and poetical fairy-story, but it was certainly written by a churchman who intended it as pious history. Purely entertainment literature, almost nonexistent in medieval Russian, becomes part of the literary scene in the seventeenth century, and is largely derived from foreign sources. Numerous examples of this exist, but it will suffice for illustrative purposes to consider only two of these, of widely different origins, which however converge in Russian to form a single genre, the more or less "chivalric" adventure story.

The well-known and very popular story of "Bova Korolevich"[5] (the youthful Pushkin started a mock epic on the subject) has its ultimate origin, so far as we know, in France, in a story about Beuve d'Antone, composed in the twelfth or thirteenth century. From France the story, like so many others, moved to Italy, where the hero became Buova d'Antona, and was rather loosely fitted into the Carolingian cycle by being made the father of the enchanter Malagigi and thus the uncle of Rinaldo of Monte Alban, his sister Bradamante, etc. Under the name of "Bevis of Hampton" Buova entered English literature in a metrical romance. The Italian version crossed the Adriatic, and via Serbia reached Belorussia, where the first known Slavic version was made. It appears that the story was known in Muscovy, perhaps through oral transmission, as early as the very beginning of the seventeenth century. Evidence for this belief is the appearance by this date of the non-Christian first name "Bova" among Muscovites. The earliest known Great Russian versions of the tale are of the late seventeenth century, and are apparently translations or adaptations from the Belorussian. By this time the original "chivalric romance" has been naturalized on Slavic soil to the point of being assimilated to native *bogatyr* traditions, and is told in a typical "fairy-tale" manner, from its traditional beginning, "In a certain kingdom, in a great lordship, in the glorious city, in Anton, lived [*zhil byl*] the famous King Vidon," etc. The usual fairy-tale manner of retarding the action by endless repetitions, very tedious to a reader, but justified in an oral presentation, prevails, and the customary "constant epithets," characteristic of folk stories, are used throughout: "white hands," "sharp spear," "steel sword," "sugary lips," "the deadly business of war" [*delo ratnoe i smertnoe*], etc. Bova's adventures begin at the age of seven, when his wicked mother, "the beautiful Militrissa" (her name is a distortion of the Italian description of her as *meretrice*, "a whore"!) tries to poison him, and he runs away to seek foreign lands. His strength and prowess are rather extraordinary. When, as a groom for King Zenzevei, he learns that an importunate suitor, King Markobrun, is coming to marry by force the beautiful Princess Druzhnevna, Bova politely requests the knightly armament necessary for battle with Markobrun, but is sensibly reminded by the Princess: "You are still a little child, only seven years from birth, and you are unable to manage a good steed, and race at a horse's full speed and swing an iron club." The young *bogatyr* accordingly saddles a palfrey, and swinging a broom, kills 15,000 of the enemy! He rescues the Princess and her father from another suitor, the *bogatyr* Lukoper, who has "a head like a beer kettle, and the eyes of the goodly man were a span apart, and between his ears you could lay a tempered arrow, and between his shoulders a *sazhen* measure, and no one under the sun was a match for him." Bova evidently doesn't belong *vo vsei podsolnichnoi* ("under the sun"), for of course, with the aid of "a goodly *bogatyr*-steed" he is more than a match for the giant. "And Lukoper could not strike through Bova's armor, but Bova struck through Lukoper's armor on both sides, and Lukoper tumbled from his horse dead, and Bova fought for 5 days and 5 nights without a let-up, and he didn't kill as many with the spear as he trampled on with his horse, and he slew 100,000 of the enemy."

At a later stage in Bova's adventures, after he has been separated from "the beautiful Princess Druzhnevna," who is now his wife, and has two sons, he wanders to the court of King Saltan Saltanovich, whose daughter, Milchigria, proposes to marry him— on condition, however, that he go over "to the Latin faith" and believe in "the god of Akhmet!" This, of course, a good Russian *bogatyr* cannot do, so he is imprisoned, but manages to escape. The tale ends with Bova reunited with his wife and family; he returns to Anton, where he cuts off the head of King Dodon (his mother's adulterer), buries his mother alive, and lives happily ever after! The last line of the manuscript announces: "And Bova's fame will not diminish for ever and ever." The prophecy seems to have been insofar fulfilled that through the nineteenth and even early twentieth centuries, chapbook versions, often illustrated with crude woodcuts, circulated the tale widely among the lower classes of Russian society.

Quite similar is the fate of the "Tale of Eruslan Lazarevich,"[6] which enjoyed popularity second only to that of "Bova." Evidently by way of the Cossack communities of the south Russian steppes, who were in contact, both friendly and hostile, with Persia, this narrative from Firdausi's famous epic the *Shah-nameh*, came to Russia. Somewhere in the line of transmission the Persian must have been translated into Turkish, for the names have been given Turkish forms. The hero of the tale is none other than Rustem (cf. Matthew Arnold's "Sohrab and Rustum"), transmogrified first into the Turkish Arslan ("lion"), then into Eruslan or Uruslan. His father's name—Persian Zal-Zar—gives the original Slavic patronymic Zalazorevich, which then becomes the more familiar Lazarevich.

There is no point in attempting to summarize the multitudinous episodes in Rustem-Eruslan's adventurous career; he is made a typical Russian *bogatyr*, in spite of the generally eastern and fabulous locale in which he moves. Among the more spectacular incidents are: his restoration of sight to his blinded father and Tsar Kirkous (Persian shah Keu-Kaws), in the course of which he encounters a gigantic severed head which conceals beneath it a magic sword; and his duel with his own unrecognized son (in the Russian version also named Uruslan), which is of course the central episode of Arnold's poem and a famous folklore motif (cf. the German *Hildebrandslied*). Another folklore motif is Uruslan's combat with a three-headed monster (*zmei*, a "dragon"), which is preparing to devour the Indian king's daughter. Uruslan's marital attachments are notably casual; he is determined to have as his wife only the most beautiful woman in the world, and heartlessly deserts one prospect after another when he learns of a more beautiful competitor. It is thus that his—presumably legal—wife, "Nastasya Barfolomeevna," the daughter of the Indian king, whom he has rescued from the dragon, bears his son after the father's departure to live with the queen of "the city of the Sun," who is unrivalled in beauty in the whole world. Reproached by his son, after their mutual recognition, for deserting his true wife and living in sin with another woman, Uruslan repents, abandons the Queen of the Sun, and returns to India. The tale ends with the son's departure to seek adventures: the young Uruslan "rode off on the clean plain (*v chistoe pole*) to go adventuring-Cossacking (*gulati-kazakovati*) on his father Uruslan's goodly steed, on the wise Arash—to seek tsars and kings and mighty *bogatyrs* and valiant men." In proper Orthodox fashion the storyteller ends his manuscript with: "Now and forever and to the ages of the ages. Amen!"

"Eruslan Lazarevich," like "Bova Korolevich," became a popular chapbook subject, and to the original adventures, numerous enough, others were added *ad libitum* in the nineteenth and early twentieth centuries. It is worth noting that this tale too has Pushkinian connections: not only is the hero of *Ruslan and Lyudmila* almost homonymous with Eruslan, but the episode of the gigantic severed—but still living—head with its concealed magic sword, which it yields to the hero so that he may exact vengeance, is taken over bodily. Ruslan encounters the head and treats it with rather arrogant disdain in Canto III of Pushkin's poem, but later receives from it the much needed magic sword.

Other similar "chivalric tales," e.g., "Peter of the Golden Keys" (the French *Pierre et Magelone*), "Tale of the Roman Emperor Otto," "Tale of Melusine," etc., mostly through Polish channels from the west, were naturalized in the seventeenth century in Russia.

In summing up this new genre of seventeenth-century Russian literature there are a number of points to be noted. First is that this is unabashed entertainment, perhaps one might even say, "escape," literature. Such a phenomenon is known to the Middle Ages only in the form of translation from other languages, and the "chivalric romance" or "adventure tale" is a translated genre. The notion of literary invention as a justified procedure was accepted only slowly and with difficulty in Russia, where it was regarded for long as a form of lying, and hence as morally reprehensible. But by way of such a western "tall tale" as that of Bova, and its assimilation with native traditions of oral storytelling, literary invention began to become legitimized.

The second fact of importance in this connection is the notable intrusion of the folkore element into the tales. Of course, such a folklore element had been there from the beginning in the western originals—enchantment, magic swords, fire-breathing dragons, and the like—and this made the interprenetration easier. And once the beginning had been made—and this genre indeed seems to be the first affected by this tendency—it was easy for other literary types, e.g., lyric poetry, to accept the infiltration of popular matter.

Third may be placed the high degree of russification of these adventure tales of very diverse origins. Elements, such as the concept of chivalry itself, which were totally alien to the Russian scene, were either eliminated or replaced by something more familiar. The "knightly code" is thus replaced by the *bogatyr's* code of honor, the steppe replaces the feudal castle as background, purely Russian customs are naively introduced, heroic names such as Bova or Uruslan are provided with patronymics, and the like. The foreign body is so thoroughly assimilated that it is hardly detectable except to a comparatist.

Finally, and particularly typical of the seventeenth century, is the almost complete absence in these tales of the ecclesiastical element, without which medieval Russian literature is all but inconceivable. Uruslan junior reproaches his father for abandonment of his "lawful" wife, and the latter acknowledges his "sin"; kings are casually mentioned as going to church, and the like; a hero refuses to abjure his religion and accept the "Latin faith." But these are all external, almost accidental, connections, in no way essential to the plot. The church and religion could be completely eliminated from these tales, and their loss would be scarcely noticeable.

F. The Picaresque Tale: "Frol Skobeev"

Literary invention, as has been noted, made its way with difficulty into original Russian artistic creation, and when it did, it masqueraded as factual truth in a way very similar to that of the Icelandic sagas, which so abound with precise proper names, dates, and the like, that an impression of overwhelming reality is created and it is very difficult to realize that, for example, the "Saga of

Burnt-Njal" is invention from beginning to end.

One of the first thoroughly "realistic" genres in European literature was created in Spain in the sixteenth century—the *picaresca*. It spread rapidly beyond the Iberian peninsula, where the first great model *(Lazarillo de Tormes)* was created by an unknown author, to England *(Jack Wilton)*, Germany *(Simplicissimus)* and France *(Gil Blas de Santillane)*. The "picaresque novel" is defined by several characteristics: it is a first person narrative, the story told by the "rogue" himself; it is episodic, without a central plot; it is satirical; it depicts real, everyday life, the lower the better; and usually, in its later representatives, but emphatically not in *Lazarillo*, it is didactic and moralistic—the "rogue" reforms and tells his story as a salutary warning.

By these criteria the "Tale of Frol Skobeev"[7] is not a genuine "picaresque novel." It is told by a third person; it has a central plot and is not episodic; the background is one of real life, but not of "low life"; it has elements of satire, but these are not dominant; and it is conspicuously without a "moral." It is quite *sui generis*, and if a genre had to be created to accommodate the tale, it would have to be called something like "a rogue's success story."

The anonymous author of "Frol Skobeev" will have been a government clerk of some sort, or possibly an impoverished nobleman of Frol Skobeev's own kind. The language is commonplace and modern, with a liberal admixture of bureaucratic jargon which points to the first hypothesis. There are several manuscripts of the "Tale," one of which gives the year 1680 as the date of the action; this would fix the date of composition at the very end of the seventeenth or beginning of the eighteenth century. The names of the protagonists of the "Tale" are genuine names of the time and place specified: there were families named Skobeev and Lovchikov in the Novgorod region around 1680. The high-ranking nobleman whose daughter Frol succeeds in seducing and marrying is named Nardin- (or Nadrin) Nashchyokin in the "Tale"; this is a fairly obvious disguise for the name of the famous diplomat of the court of Alexei Mikhailovich, Afanasy Lavrentevich Ordyn-Nashchyokin, who negotiated the Treaty of Andrusovo with Poland, among many other services to his Tsar. It is not impossible that some of the "Tale" may have a factual basis. Certainly at least the general atmosphere of cynical determination to "get ahead" at all costs is true to the times, and the social picture, typified by Frol, of the displacement of an old and conservative *boyar* aristocracy by a pushing and vulgar lower stratum of service gentry *(dvoriane)* coincides precisely with what we know otherwise of the reign of Peter the Great's father.

Frol Skobeev, a poor *dvorianin* of the Novgorod Province and neighbor of an estate owned by the *stolnik* ("gentleman-waiter" —a very high court rank) Nardin-Nashchyokin determines to become the latter's son-in-law and thus make his fortune. At a time when Nardin-Nashchyokin's daughter Annushka and her nurse are in residence at their Novgorod estate, and the girl's parents are in Moscow, Frol puts his plan into operation. Annushka gives a party for the neighborhood girls, and Frol's sister is invited. Frol dresses as a girl and accompanies his sister to the party. At a convenient moment during the evening he reveals himself to Annushka's nurse and with a generous bribe wins her cooperation in his scheme. The nurse proposes a "game such as she used to play in her youth," which is that Annushka should play "bride" and Frol (in his girl's disguise) play "bridegroom." Everything proceeds smoothly, and the "bride" and "groom" are duly sent to bed together. Frol has no trouble in seducing Annushka, and the girl enjoys the situation so much that she keeps the disguised Frol in her house for several days. Her protests to the nurse over the latter's part in the seduction are extremely perfunctory; Annushka ends with, "Well, nurse, let it be this way, for never again shall I regain my chastity."

Nardin-Nashchyokin then sends for his daughter to join him in Moscow, and the girl has to leave her lover. Skobeev, however, follows her. His farewell words to his sister are quite revealing: "Well, my dear sister, don't grieve about anything. Though I should lose my life, I won't leave Annushka until my life ends. I shall be either a colonel *(polkovnik)* or a dead man *(pokoinik)*!" He finds quarters in Moscow near the Nardin-Nashchyokin house, and at church manages to get in touch with the accommodating nurse, who again manages the details. She tells Frol that Annushka's aunt, who is a nun at the Novodevichy convent, has invited her niece to visit her, and will send a carriage for her. Frol then induces a nobleman "friend" of his, Lovchikov (another *stolnik* and a friend of Nardin-Nashchyokin) to lend him his carriage and footman "in order to fetch his bride." Again everything works out according to plan; Annushka leaves her father's house in the borrowed carriage, goes to her lover, and they are married. For some time the father is unaware of the situation; it is not until he visits his sister and inquires about his daughter that he learns the truth—Annushka has disappeared! The aggrieved nobleman complains to the Tsar, who proclaims a dire punishment for Annushka's abductor. Frol then goes to Lovchikov, tells him the whole story, and demands his assistance, under threat of revealing him as an accomplice if he refuses. Lovchikov then intervenes with Nardin-Nashchyokin, who after his first explosion of anger, realizes that nothing can be done to remedy the situation, and he had best accept it. At first he refuses all communication with his daughter and "that rascal Skobeev," his unwanted son-in-law; but eventually Frol's wiles bring around both parents, and the "Tale" ends "happily" (for Frol and Annushka) with reconciliation and the gift of a large and remunerative estate.

One of the most significant aspects of the story is the total absence of moral scruple on the parts of Frol himself, of Annushka, and most of all, of the nurse. Frol is ruthlessly determined to "make his fortune," and has no hesitation about using bribery, rape and blackmail to this end; Annushka lets herself be seduced by the disguised "bridegroom" with remarkable ease, abandons her father and mother to follow him with callous indifference, and cooperates with Frol in the trick by which relations are finally restored with her family. And the nurse, for a few rubles, agrees first to provide her "benefactor" with the perfect opportunity for ravishing her mistress; and then contrives the plot for Annushka's abduction. Never throughout the "Tale" is there any indication that any of the actors in it is moved by moral considerations, either of scruple against roguery or of repentance after it. And even more noticeably, no reprehension is expressed by the author over their actions. Here is no "exemplary tale," with justice overcoming ill conduct, but quite the contrary. The reader is left at the end with the edifying picture of a pair of thoroughly amoral rascals rewarded by honor and wealth. Even the nurse suffers no punishment for her double-dealing.

From the stylistic point of view, the "Tale of Frol Skobeev," in spite of its rather commonplace and vulgar language, is notable for its vividness of characterization, which is particularly enhanced by the considerable amount of very lifelike direct discourse. A particularly good example of this is afforded by the dialogue between Nardin-Nashchyokin and his sister when the former inquires about Annushka:

He was there for some time without seeing his daugher, and asked his sister: "Sister, why don't I see Annushka?" And his sister answered him: "Stop joking, brother! What am I to do, when I'm unlucky in my request? I asked you to send her to me; evidently you aren't willing to trust me, and I haven't the time to send for her." And the *stolnik* Nardin-Nashchyokin said to his sister: "What, my lady and sister, are you talking about? I don't understand you, because she was sent to you a month ago, because you sent a carriage with horses for her! I was on a visit at the time with my wife, and at my orders she was permitted to go to you." And his sister said to him: "Never, brother, did I send horses and carriage! Annushka hasn't been with me!" And *stolnik* Nardin-Nashchyokin began to grieve greatly for his daughter, and wept bitterly, because his daughter had vanished without a trace.

The "Tale of the Nobleman Frol Skobeev" is one of the three high points of Russian seventeenth-century literature, and like the other two ("The Tale of Sorrow-Misfortune") and the "Life of the Archpriest Avvakum Written by Himself") is unique in its kind. The few other "real life" tales coming from the century, e.g. the "Tale of Karp Sutulov," are either naturalized imports or satires with little attempt at characterization.

G. *The Satirical Tale: "Yorsh Yorshovich" and "Shemyaka's Judgment"*

The satirical bent has always been an inherent feature of Russian popular literature, and it sometimes takes the form of parody. This is the case with a piece ordinarily known as "The Tale of Yorsh Yorshovich."[8] "Tale" is a misnomer: the manuscript title more accurately reflects the nature of the piece—"Transcript, word for word, of the court action, how Bream got judgment on Ruff." The piece is a very close parody of contemporary legal procedure, and its evident familiarity with the *Ulozhenie* of Tsar Alexei Mikhailovich (promulgated in 1649) makes it likely that it was composed not long after the middle of the seventeenth century. The author would have been, very likely, some minor legal officer.

In form the parody professes to be a transcript of the proceedings arising from a suit brought by the fish Bream, a nobleman *(boiarskii syn)* of Lake Rostov, against the fish Ruff, son of Ruff (Yorsh Yorshovich), of the family of Pricklers *(Shchetiniki)*. The plaintiff begins: "My Lords Fishes, great Sturgeon *[Osiotr]* and Beluga and Whiting *[belaia rybitsa]*, Bream *[Leshch]*, humble nobleman of Rostov Lake, with his comrades, makes obeisance. Our complaint, my Lords, is against the low-born person *[zloi chelovek]* Ruff Prickler, the rogue. In years past, my Lords, Rostov Lake belonged to us; but this Ruff, this low-born person, heir of the Pricklers, has deprived us of Rostov Lake, our ancient perquisite." Bream then goes on to accuse Ruff of using his prickles offensively against the Bream family, who are decent, law-abiding citizens. Ruff is called upon to make his defence, which he does as follows:

In answer, my Lords, for myself and my comrades, I state that Rostov Lake was the ancestral property of our grandfathers, and now ours; and he, Bream, lived in our neighborhood on the lake bottom, and didn't use to come out into the light. But I, Ruff, my Lords, by God's grace, my father's blessing and my mother's prayers, am no rioter nor brigand nor thief nor robber. I have never been in custody, I have never had stolen articles confiscated from me, I am a person of quality *[dobryi chelovek]*, I live by my own efforts, not those of others; I am known in Moscow and other great cities by princes and boyars, gentlemen-waiters and noblemen, Moscow burghers, secretaries *[diaki]* and clerks *[pod''iachie]* and people of all ranks. They buy me for a high price and bake me with pepper and saffron, and serve me honorably, and many people of quality eat me after a hangover, and congratulate me after having eaten.

The judges then call on the plaintiff with the words: "Whom do you have with knowledge of Rostov Lake and the rivers and springs and on whom do you call?" The plaintiff replies: "I call,

my Lords, on the people of quality of various towns and districts; there is, my Lords, a person of quality who lives in the German district under Ivan-gorod [a town on the Finnish Gulf] in the river Narva, by name Whitefish *[sig]*, and a second person of quality, my Lords, who lives in the Novgorod district in the river Volkhov, by name fish Loduga [?]." To these witnesses the defendant objects on the grounds that they, like Bream himself, are "wealthy people, well endowed with goods." The court then requests the plaintiff to name another witness, which he does—the Herring (*sel'd'*) of Pereslavl. Again Ruff objects: "Whitefish and Loduga and Herring and their kin, and Bream is just the same sort of wealthy person: they live as neighbors, where they resort to the law—they eat and drink together, and have no word about us."

At this point the judges send out the bailiff Perch (*okun'*) with orders to subpoena as witnesses Burbot (*mnia*) and Herring. Burbot, however, "promises bailiff Perch great bribes" and begs off from serving: "Lord Perch! I am not fit to be a witness; I have a big belly—I can't walk, and my eyes are small, I can't see far, and my lips are thick—I can't talk before quality people!" So the bailiff subpoenas instead Dace (*golavl'*) and Carp (*iaz'*) and Herring. Herring is called on for testimony, which is as follows: "Bream and his comrades are right; Bream is a person of quality, a godly Christian, he lives by his own and not by another's [efforts], while Ruff, my lords, is a person of low quality, a Prickler."

At this point the manuscripts become confused; there are two different recensions of the proceedings, differing very widely in characterization, and it is apparent that there has been a contamination of the two here. Sturgeon, who is at the beginning of the piece one of the judges, now comes forward as a witness for the prosecution, and tells a heart-rending story of how he, "an old muzhik," has been twice deceived by Ruff, the second time by being lured into a dragnet from which he is hauled out on the ground and beaten by the fisherman, while Ruff looks on and calls ironically: "Brother Sturgeon, endure for Christ's sake!"

The trial ends with the verdict that Ruff is guilty, and the sentence of death is passed. "Says Ruff to the judges: 'My Lords Judges! You have judged not according to justice, but according to bribes! You have upheld Bream and his comrades and condemned me.' Ruff spat in the eyes of the judges and jumped into

56

the bushes. That was the last they saw of Ruff."

In the "Tale" there is the humor that derives from the use of animals in human parts—the same sort of thing as is familiar to the West in the story of "Reynard the Fox," in its innumerable versions. There is a certain amount of satirical point in various of the legal episodes, especially of course, in the bribery of bailiff Perch. But the most startling aspect of the satire is the manner in which the same situation is used in the two different versions to apply to two entirely different social conditions. In the first, except for the strange intrusion of Sturgeon's testimony, which comes from the second, Yorsh Yorshovich is another Frol Skobeev, an impudent, pushing, cheating commoner, against whose aggression the somewhat stupid well-to-do upperclass fish are helpless. Ruff is the representative of the lower classes, and his challenge of the testimony of Bream's witnesses on the grounds of their class solidarity with the plaintiff is felt to be thoroughly justified. But in the second version, which appears elsewhere independently and fully, and is apparently a later one, and which in the Zabelin manuscript introduces such a discordant note by transforming Sturgeon from a judge to a witness, Ruff is an arrogant nobleman, Bream and Sturgeon are "peasants" (note that Sturgeon calls himself a *staryi muzhik*), and the court *acquits* Ruff, obviously influenced by bribes.. Thus the satire of court corruption and the helplessness of the "little man" against the powerful and well-connected nobleman works in opposite directions in the two versions.

To complete the account of this popular parody I can do no better than quote the words of V.P. Adrianova-Peretts and D.S. Likhachev from the preface of their edition of *Russian Democratic Poetry of the Seventeenth Century*[9] on the subject of a popular versified redaction of the "Tale":

To the second half of the seventeenth century is dated also the rhymed "Tale of Yorsh," which represents a reworking of a widespread satirical tale—the lawsuit of the ruff and the bream, which tells how the ruff, having escaped the court sentence, is caught, prepared, and made into fish soup. The whole little tale is built up on play with rhymes and assonances on proper names—a device widely employed in proverbs and proverbial expressions. . . . The tale could continue to grow until the composer's inventiveness was exhausted, stringing together ever new names with their chiming words. It is just from the point of view of this playing with rhymes and chimes that the little tale is interesting, confirming the taste of seventeenth-century democratic circles

57

for rhymed discourse.

Parody of solemn officialese was a popular genre in seventeenth-century Russia, and besides the case of Yorsh Yorshovich other legal parodies are known, such as the "Petition of Kalyazin Monastery,"[10] which is precisely dated to the year 1677. It takes the form of a petition from the monks of Kalyazin to the Archbishop of Tver, complaining of the unreasonable conduct of their Archimandrite Gavriil. The Archimandrite insists on having bells rung at inconvenient hours in the evening and disturbing the brothers' sleep; they are forced to interrupt their serious business of drinking beer in order to sing masses; a guard is placed at the monastery gate who won't let them out to go begging and wenching in the nearby villages, etc. The petition ends with the dire threat that if Archimandrite Gavriil does not mend his ways, the entire community will desert the monastery and find another more attuned to their mode of life. There is a parody of the popular medical treatises of the day, entitled: "Medical Handbook on How to Treat Foreigners," and there are even some parodies on the church service, e.g. "Holiday Mass of the Tavern Idlers," and on saints' lives, e.g. "Legend of the Peasant's Son." In the "Holiday Mass" the object of the satire is not merely the drunken life of the peasants, but the government policy of encouraging alcoholic consumption in order to increase revenue. In the "Legend" a dissolute youth breaks into a peasant's storehouse at night, and as he steals one article after another, utters appropriate quotations from Scripture or the Mass; thus, as he eats a loaf of the peasant's bread, he recites a part of the Communion service: "Receive the body of Christ, taste of the fount immortal." When at his wife's insistence the peasant goes out to intercept the thief, and hits him on the head with a cudgel, the thief quotes the Psalter: "Sprinkle me with hyssop and I shall be cleansed and become whiter than snow." The peasant is convinced that he has killed an angel and retires to reproach his wife for leading him into mortal sin, while the thief makes off with all his movable property.[11]

Satire of institutions and social mores of the time was not confined, however, to the form of parody. Another satirical genre is that of the short narrative, illustrating a social abuse. Such is the well-known "Shemyaka's Judgment" (Shemiakin sud),[12] which became very popular and was perpetuated in the eighteenth

58

century in chapbook form, with woodcuts. The original of the story is an eastern "wandering tale," and the Russian name of the corrupt judge seems to be derived from that of a factious nobleman of the fifteenth century, Dmitry Shemyaka, the cousin and enemy of Tsar Vasily II. The tale has two points, both indicative of a popular inspiration: the venality of the judge, presumably typical of the entire judicial system; and the triumph of the "poor man" whom the corrupt judge exonerates by mistake.

There were two brothers, one rich and one poor. The poor man tries his rich brother's patience by constantly asking for loans, and so when he goes to request his brother to lend him his horse to draw firewood from the forest, the rich brother lends the horse but refuses the harness. The poor brother accordingly ties his load of wood to the horse's tail, and in straining to drag the load, the horse pulls off his own tail. When the poor man returns the tailless horse, his brother refuses to accept it, and takes the matter to court. As plaintiff and defendant make their way to town together, they put up at the house of a village priest for the night. The priest assigns the poor man to sleep on a *polaty*, a kind of flimsy wooden loft between the ceiling of a peasant house and the top of the stove. The poor man peers down from this perch at the priest and his brother feasting; the loft breaks and he falls upon the priest's baby son and kills him. The priest accordingly joins the rich brother in bringing action against the poor man. As the trio approach the town, they have to cross a bridge high over a sort of dry ditch. The poor man, despairing of his situation, decides to end it all, and jumps from the bridge. Instead of breaking his own neck, however, he falls on a sick man whose son is driving him to the baths, and kills him. Another plaintiff is thus added to the original two. The poor man, before going into court, picks up a stone, wraps it in his handkerchief, and puts it in his hat.

Judge Shemyaka hears the first testimony and asks the poor brother for his defense. Having none to make, the latter simply takes off his hat, mutely exhibits the wrapped stone, and bows. Supposing the bundle to be a bag of money being offered as a bribe, Shemyaka then renders judgment: the horse is to remain with the poor man until he grows a new tail, at which time the rich brother can have him back. The second case follows the same pattern: again the defense consists of the gesture with the "money bag," and the sentence is: the priest shall surrender his wife to the poor

59

man until she produces a new baby to replace the dead one. In the last case, similarly decided, the son is directed to hurl himself from the bridge upon the poor man standing beneath, and requite him thus for the father's death. None of the plaintiffs is satisfied with the verdict, and all pay the poor man in order to avoid compliance. Finally a messenger from Shemyaka arrives to ask the acquitted poor man for what he carried in his bundle. Taking the stone out of the handkerchief the poor man says he intended to give it to the judge (i.e., hit him with it) if he had rendered an unfavorable verdict. On hearing this Shemyaka gives thanks to God that he had decided the case as he had! "The poor man, however, went to his home rejoicing."

Other "wandering tales," in one form or another, became part of seventeenth-century Russia's repertory of satire. Such, for example, is the "Fable [Pritcha] of the Old Husband,"[13] who, in spite of all the dire and insulting warnings of the young girl whom he woos, marries her and is properly subjected to all the indignities which she has promised him. Some of the tales have a notably irreverent attitude toward religion: thus, in the fable of "The Fox and the Cock,"[14] the latter, who because of his fine voice is a subdeacon, is unable to save his life when caught by the fox in spite of his apt quotations of Scripture; the fox can also quote Holy Writ, and condemns the victim for contentiousness with his brothers and polygamy. In the "Fable of the Drunkard"[15] (from an Old French fabliau) the drunkard's soul goes to heaven and knocks at the gate. One after another various saints and patriarchs inform him that drunkards are not allowed in heaven, but as the petitioner learns the identity of each interlocutor, he reproaches him with some well-known failing of his own and puts him to shame. Thus, Peter's threefold denial of Christ, St. Paul's stoning of St. Stephen, David's adultery with Bathsheba, etc., are evidently more serious sins than drunkenness. When finally St. John the Divine appears at the gate, the drunkard reminds him: "You and Luke wrote in the Gospel: 'Love one another,' and God loves all. But you hate the newcomer, and you hate me! John the Divine! Either you are belying your hand [i.e., what you have written], or else open [i.e., explain] the words!" John the Divine says: "You are our man, drunkard! Enter into our Paradise!" This tale disturbed church authorities enough so that it was placed on a list of forbidden books.

H. The Autobiography: "Life of Archpriest Avvakum, Written by Himself"

As was mentioned above in connection with the "Tale of Frol Skobeev," the three outstanding masterpieces of seventeenth-century Russian literature are each unique in their kinds. One of the highest points in this literature is *The Life of Archpriest Avvakum, Written by Himself.*[16] Autobiography is a genre known to earlier Russian literature only in the—again unique—example of what is usually called "The Testament of Vladimir Monomakh," from the twelfth century. The author of the seventeenth-century autobiography is a famous leader of the Old Ritualists, Avvakum (i.e., Habbakuk) Petrovich (1621-1682).

The Autobiography of Archpriest Avvakum is a great piece of literature, and in its highly original style one of the best evidences for the "emancipation of personality" which Professor Likhachev regards as the distinctive mark of the seventeenth century. An appreciation and understanding of this work, however, are rendered difficult by the author's inextricable involvement in some of the most confusing events of his age, and an at least brief account of these events has to be prefixed to a consideration of the *Autobiography* as literature.

The reign of Tsar Alexei Mikhailovich (1645-1676) is in many respects as crucial in Russian history as that of his more spectacular son Peter (1683-1725). The famous "westernization" by Peter had its modest beginnings in the earlier reign, and the consolidation of autocracy which culminated in the "Empire" proclaimed by Peter was carried well along under Tsar Alexei.

The aspect of the reign which concerns Avvakum and to

which this exposition will confine itself is the ecclesiastical policy and career of Patriarch Nikon. In the tortuous confusion of contradictions involving the relations between Tsar, Patriarch and Archpriest we may well attempt first to clarify the personal motives of the three men. Tsar Alexei Mikhailovich was a well-educated and generally enlightened monarch, whose surface mildness concealed a strong will and great obstinacy. Although personally attracted by aspects of western culture, for example the theater, he publicly maintained the image of old Muscovite piety. He strengthened the position of the gentry *(dvoriane)* who were the support of his own power through legislation (the *Ulozhenie* of 1649) which to all intents and purposes terminated the evolution of the free peasantry *(krest'ianstvo)* into serfs, and his government ruthlessly suppressed the several popular uprisings that occurred in his reign (e.g. that of Stepan Razin, 1669-71) as a result of the people's resentment at this change in their condition. Tsar Alexei's foreign policy was expansionist: he accepted the union of the Ukraine with Muscovy (1654) and fought Poland to maintain this acquisition. He dreamed of making the Orthodox Russian Tsardom the heir in Constantinople of the defunct Byzantine Empire, and of gathering all the Orthodox subjects of the Turks into the Russian fold. In the interests of conciliating the Ukraine, which was partially Catholic (since the "Union" of 1595) he wanted to reform the rather lax mode of life of much of the Russian clergy, and introduce western (Latin) learning; and in order to attract the Greeks to his dream of a Russian protectorate he was anxious to bring the ritual and usages of the Russian church into conformity with Greek practices, from which minor discrepancies had developed in the course of centuries. For both these ecclesiastical ends he actively encouraged a reform movement which began apparently independently within the Russian church, led by the so-called "zealots for piety." The "zealots," among whom were Nikon, then archimandrite of the New St. Savior Monastery in Moscow, archpriest Ivan Neronov of the Kazan Cathedral in Moscow, and his protégé the provincial archpriest Avvakum, who had already made a name for himself as a champion of puritanism in his home village and later parishes, began their activities with measures designed to eliminate drunkenness, secular entertainments, sexual immorality, and other abuses among the people, and in particular the clergy.

Nikon was a peasant's son, but very well educated; personally tall and impressive, with a magnetic charm which he used effectively on the Tsar, he was motivated by an enormous ambition, perhaps more for the Church than for himself. Having become favorably known to the Tsar, Nikon had a meteoric rise; he was appointed Archbishop of Novgorod in 1649, and when Patriarch Iosif died in 1652, the Tsar obtained his election as Patriarch. Unquestionably Nikon was genuinely concerned with the low state of clerical morality, and joined with fervor in the efforts of the "zealots" to combat this. He was also, it seems, convinced of the necessity for the Russian church to abandon its ingrained suspicion and hostility toward western learning, represented by the Ukrainian seminary of Kiev, where Latin was taught, and of the desirability of eliminating the minor differences in church ritual and in the church books between the Greek and the Russian branches of the Orthodox church. In both respects Nikon's position coincided with that of the Tsar. The same was not true, however, of Nikon's most fundamental conviction. This domineering and inflexible man had come to hold a belief similar to those of Pope Boniface VIII in the west and of Michael Cerularius in eleventh-century Byzantium—that the ecclesiastical power was divinely ordained to be superior, or at least equal to, the temporal. Nikon was determined to render the Russian church, which from the days of St. Vladimir had always been almost an organ of the secular government, independent and answerable only to God. Here was the rock on which the amicable relations between Patriarch and Tsar finally foundered; Nikon was removed from office in 1660 and condemned a few years later by the Church Council of 1666 to spend the rest of his life as a simple monk in his favorite monastery, the New Jerusalem.

When we come to Avvakum we are faced with an even greater combination of contradictions than in the cases of the Tsar and the Patriarch. Born in 1621 to a parish priest in the district of Nizhny Novgorod, Avvakum had the kind of education which his position made natural—purely ecclesiastical. He married at 17, and passed rapidly from the diaconate to ordination as a priest. Avvakum was a man, as all his writings make evident, fully deserving of the epithets "mutinous" and "turbulent" which his enemies applied to him. In every post which he ever held, whether in the provinces or in Moscow, including the parish priesthood in his own native village, he made himself so obnoxious, not only to the "authorities," but to his common parishioners, that he was persecuted and driven out. His house was even burned on one occasion. These extreme reactions must have been occasioned by his intemperate and violent attempts to reform what he regarded as "abuses." He was a man of absolutely unbending will, determined, as he said himself, "to die for a single A." His reform activities in the provinces brought him to the Tsar's notice, and he was brought to Moscow, where he cooperated briefly with the "zealots" and Nikon. When, however, Nikon in 1653 promulgated a decree for the reform of Russian church ritual and church books, Avvakum was stunned, and reacted with his usual violence. From 1653 dates the "Raskol," or "Schism" in the Russian Orthodox Church and the formation of the sect of "Old Ritualists." Avvakum was the spiritual leader of the movement.

The position which Avvakum and his friend Ivan Neronov and their followers took requires some explanation. Russian Christianity was from the outset marked by an extreme formalism. With the exception, of course, of some of the better educated upper clergy, believers regarded the divine liturgy as a species of incantation, the efficacy of which for ensuring salvation depended upon a punctilious exactitude of performance. Even the slightest deviation from the traditional forms might vitiate the entire procedure. At the same time most Russian circles harbored a deep and unreasoning hatred of the Latin "heresy" of Roman Catholicism, and the conviction, historically formulated in the famous doctrine of the "three Romes," that because of its fatal submission to union with Catholicism at the Council of Florence-Ferrara in 1439, the "second Rome," Constantinople, had forfeited God's grace forever and been condignly punished for its apostasy by the Turkish conquest of 1453. Thenceforth the only Orthodox center in the world was the "third Rome," Moscow—"And a fourth there will not be."

In all probability Patriarch Nikon and the Tsar had no suspicion that the proclamation of 1653 would arouse such an embittered opposition. The changes involved were almost ridiculously trivial—whether the name of Jesus should be spelled in Russian with one "i" or two; the number of prostrations to be made and of "halleluiahs" to be sung at different portions of the Mass; and the number of fingers to be used in making the sign of the Cross—

three, as the Greek usage was, to symbolize the Trinity, or two, to symbolize Christ's dual nature. But the reformers failed to realize the degree to which such custom-consecrated matters were a part of the very fabric of Russian Orthodoxy, and how a change in them would seem to the faithful a dangerous concession to the hated Roman church and an abandonment of Moscow's proud position as head of the Orthodox Church in favor of the discredited Greeks. Thus a combination of superstitious literalism and of an outraged sentiment of national superiority provoked the extraordinary reaction of the Schismatics, and their leader, Avvakum.

Marxist historians, who must always look for the "real" causes of a spiritual or intellectual movement in contemporary economic and social conditions, find them here in the discontent of all the classes of Muscovite society, except the service gentry and the bureaucracy, with the increasingly centralized and autocratic government. The loss of their last vestiges of liberty by the peasantry, and the rapid worsening of their lot under the oppression of the landholding gentry, the privileged monasteries, and the State itself, led to numerous flare-ups of social protest, both among the rural agriculturists and the small artisans of the towns; and many of the lower clergy, both "white" (i.e., the parish priests) and "black" (i.e., the monks), because of their own peasant origin and close association with the populace, made common cause with the protesters. At the same time the relatively small middle class of town merchants, aggrieved by crushing taxation, government restrictions on trade, and the favoritism which the government exhibited toward foreigners (*nemtsy*—"Germans," i.e. Teutons, including Hollanders and Englishmen), were attracted at first toward an anti-governmental movement. Most surprising of all was the support which the Raskol derived from some of the old aristocracy, the boyars. Since the terrible days of Ivan IV's *oprichnina* the boyar class had lost its position almost entirely to the upstart service gentry (*dvorianstvo*). For such a group, proud and smarting from their humiliation, the Raskol offered the refuge of a kind of Russian "Fronde." The numbers of such dissidents were not great, but they gave the movement prestige. It must be remembered that after Avvakum and his two followers who were burned with him at the stake in 1682, the most important martyrs of the early movement were the boyarina Morozova and the boyarina Urusova, who died in prison.

No western historian would be likely to accept the Marxist interpretation of the religious issues in the Raskol as mere disguises, even if unconscious, for the "real" economic and social causation; but there can be no question of the importance of the latter factors in the massive original support which the religious Schism, once begun, attracted. There can be no question, either, of the fragility of the anti-governmental movement, the supporters of which had no community of interests beyond religious conservatism to hold them together. There is no surprise in the collapse of the Raskol and its degeneration into a persecuted minority, mostly of peasants and small traders, pushed into the wildest and most inhospitable regions of Russia, but maintaining its stubborn resistance to the very end of the Tsardom—and beyond.

To return to our literary subject, Archpriest Avvakum Petrovich. His refusal to bow to the authority of the Church, vested in its head, the Patriarch, resulted in several imprisonments, and exile to Siberia, where he was accompanied by his wife and children. Everywhere he went he preached his appeal to resist the Nikonian innovations, and achieved the status of a saint and martyr in the eyes of the common people. When Tsar Alexei and his Patriarch parted company on the matter of church independence, in 1660, the Tsar recalled Avvakum from exile, hoping to win him as an ally against the still popular Nikon. It should be noted that Alexei did not by any means repudiate what Nikon had accomplished in church reformation, which as has been pointed out, coincided with the Tsar's own interests; the Patriarch was deposed on grounds of insubordination to his secular master. Consequently Avvakum, inalterably opposed to the Nikonian innovations, which were still in effect, now opposed the Tsar, who supported them, just as resolutely. He was again exiled, this time to north Russia, to a desolate prison in the tundra at Pustozersk. Here he remained from 1667 to 1682, living in the most appalling conditions, deprived of every necessity, but continuing to preach his cause now for the first time through his writings, which the hordes of pilgrims to his prison disseminated far and wide through Russia. When Tsar Alexei died, in 1676, Avvakum addressed a "petition" to his son and successor Tsar Fyodor, in which he warned the new Tsar that his father was now in Hell, suffering for his abandonment of the true faith. Fyodor, although personally a

66

gentle and sickly young man, averse to violence, let his counselors persuade him that Avvakum was a dangerous menace to the State, and the obdurate old man and three of his closest associates were burned at the stake on the 14th of April, 1682, for "high treason against the house of the Tsar."

There are about eighty of Avvakum's writings extant—a tribute to the assiduity and devotion of his followers in preserving and copying them. There are letters, petitions, sermons, and polemics; and there is, of greatest literary interest, the famous "Autobiography" (*Zhitie protopopa Avvakuma, im samim napisannoe*, or "Life of Archpriest Avvakum, Written by Himself"). There are three versions of this, of dates between 1672 and 1676. One manuscript of the first version is in Avvakum's own hand.

"Autobiography," as we have noted before, is a genre of writing unknown to the Middle Ages. The individual during this period was submerged in the group, and it would have been considered the height of presumption and sinful pride to make one's own life the subject of a literary composition. What motivated Avvakum to break with this convention must remain hidden for us, but in view of the attitude often revealed in the *Autobiography* and of the genre which served more often than any other as a model for it, i.e., the "Saint's Life," it may be conjectured that the author actually considered himself a saint and martyr for the faith. His *Life*, like those composed about recognized saints of the church, is rife with miracles (e.g. Avvakum's feeding by an angel—with a tasty cabbage soup, incidentally!); he has prophetic visions; he is directly attacked by the Devil, etc. To be sure, he recognizes his own sinfulness and fallibility, and even upbraids himself at times for presumption, as when, on the journey to Dauria, he befriends a couple of widows and thereby incurs the hostility of the governor Pashkov, who has him flogged:

But now, as I lay, the thought came to me: "Son of God, why didst thou permit them to beat me so sorely? Look thee, Lord, I was championing the widow, consecrated to thee. Who shall judge between me and thee? When I was living as an evil man, thou didst not chastise me thus; but now I know not in what I have sinned." Ay! There was a righteous man for you, another dung-faced Pharisee, wishing, forsooth, to judge the Almighty![17]

But there is no question in his mind of his own absolute rightness in defending the old ways, and the absolute and damnable heresy of Nikon and the other "reformers." And he evidently sees nothing un-Christian about cursing and reviling his enemies in the most outrageous and unseemly language.

The "saint's life," then, is Avvakum's chief model for his great pioneering work; and to this must be added the medieval homily, for interpolated through the *Life* are numerous exhortations on doctrinal matters, and the general intent of the writing in the first place is clearly to strengthen the faithful in time of persecution, through the recital of the author's own steadfastness. In attempting to define the genre of Avvakum's masterpiece, the Soviet critic V.E. Gusev sums up his conclusions: "In essence the 'Life' is a real-life autobiographical account, with a multitude of characters, tending to a significant degree toward the large form of the novel."[18]

Constructionally a "Life," whether one's own or another's, offers a ready-made framework which it is not easy to alter. Avvakum begins with his birth, family, early education, etc., and proceeds chronologically to his imprisonment at Pustozersk. Some episodes receive a good deal more attention than others, and for a modern reader by far the most engrossing part of the *Life* is the account of the travels in Siberia, first to Tobolsk, then to Dauria (east of Lake Baikal), and finally back to Moscow. Certainly the secret of Avvakum's literary mastery is the direct, vivid portrayal of the most ordinary details of life. Nothing could be farther than this procedure from the traditional "saint's life" formula, with its schematized and "universal" background, and its florid and artificial language. Where else in early Russian literature, for example, could one find such a passage as this?[19]

And we had a pet, a black hen, and she laid two eggs a day to feed the children, by God's will, helping us in our need; it was God's doing. But when they were carrying out the baggage to the dog sledge, she was crushed to death, for our sins, and to this day whenever I think of that hen my heart aches for her. I know not if it were a hen or a miracle: all the year round she laid two eggs a day, and we would not have taken a hundred rubles for her—nay, we would have spat on them! mere dross! And that hen, God's living creature, fed us, and she would take her meals with us, pecking at the porridge of fir cones in the cauldron, and pecking at the fish, and in exchange she gave us two eggs a day. Glory to God, who fashions all things well!

Avvakum is a writer of the most violent contrasts, and one might perhaps see in this aspect of his personality a feature of the "Baroque," if it were not that it is so obviously an inseparable aspect of his own personality and utterly free of literary artifice. As he says, "I am untaught in rhetoric and in philosophy." After the sweet humanism of the story of the little black hen, one reads with a sense of shocked disbelief the merciless diatribes which Avvakum hurls at the Nikonians, as for example:[20]

And they have planned with the devil to misprint books and falsify everything, and to alter the sign of the cross in church, and on the wafers. Within the altar they have banished the priestly prayers, they have altered the "Lord have mercy upon us," and in baptism they bid to invoke the Evil One. I would fain spit in his eyes and in theirs! And round about the font the Evil One leads them against the course of the sun, and in like fashion they consecrate the church, and when they solemnize marriage they lead the married counterclockwise; plainly they do this in hostility. And in baptism they do not abjure the Evil One. How should they? They are his children and they do not desire to abjure their father. But why multiply words? Woe is me for the True Believer! Every spirit that is exalted is brought low. As Nikon, the hound of hell, spake, so did he do. . . . It behooves every man to endure for this, even unto death. May these damnable ones be accursed, with all their devilish imaginations: and to them whom they have made to suffer in their souls, may theirs be threefold eternal remembrance.

But just before this passage Avvakum has been pleading for religious toleration:

They think to establish the faith by fire or the knout and gallows-tree. Which of the Apostles taught them that? I know not. My Christ did not teach his Apostles that fire and knout and gallows-tree should lead to the faith. . . . The Tatar god Mahmud in his books wrote thus: "We bid you lay low with the sword the heads of them that obey not our law and tradition." But Christ never gave such like command to his disciples.[21]

Something of the contradiction in Avvakum comes out in this passage—the appeal to Christ and His Apostles, who preached love and gentleness, side by side with the assignment of Nikon and his innovators to eternal hell fire—because they would change the direction of religious processions and the words used in the ritual of baptism!

The violence of contrast is evident throughout Avvakum's work: in theological doctrine, as in the above; in the alternating pictures of saints and sinners; and even in the nature of his language. The *Life* is an extraordinary and entirely idiosyncratic mélange of the conventional Russo-Slavonic, normal in a "saint's life," with the most earthy, plebeian vernacular, such as had rarely before even found itself in print. The effect of such a juxtaposition is hard to convey in translation, since English knows no such hierarchies of language. Avvakum can curse his enemies like a fishwife, in the vulgarest of terms, and in the next breath create an exalted atmosphere with Biblical language, quoted or echoed. Thus in his account of one of his earlier affrays with enraged parishioners, Avvakum begins:[22] "But a little time thereafter others once again drove me out of that place" (*pomale paki inii izgnasha mia ot mesta togo vdrugoriad*). Except for the phrase "out of that place" (*ot mesta togo*) every word in the sentence is Church Slavonic; and most noticeable of all is the obsolete aorist tense *izgnasha* ("drove out") and the monosyllabic form of the personal pronoun *mia* ("me"). A sentence or two later he writes: "And there I lived for a little while—only eight weeks; the Devil instructed the priests and the peasant men and peasant women—they came to the Patriarch's chancellery, where I was doing church business, and dragging me away from the chancellery in a mob—there must have been about 1500 of them—they beat me with sticks in the midst of the street and trampled on me." Here all the verbs without exception—seven of them—are the so-called "compound past tense" that is normal in modern Russian, and was normal in spoken use in the seventeenth century—*pozhil, nauchil, prishli, delal*, etc. The pronoun "I" in this passage is the ordinary Russian *ia* (in the immediately preceding sentence he has used the Slavonic *az*), and the accusative case of the same pronoun here is the Russian *menia* instead of the Slavonic *mia* used above. Even the adverb "a little" has been changed, from the Slavonic *pomale* to the Russian *nemnogo*. And only a few lines further on he quotes the outraged people of Yurevich-Povolsky, whom he had reproved "for their whoring (*bliudni*)" as shouting to each other: "Kill the rascal, the son of a bitch (*bliudina syna*), and throw his body in the ditch for the dogs!" The word "whore," it may be noted (modern Russian *bliad'*) is even today never printed, but indicated by dashes!

When V.E. Gusev remarks that Avvakum's "autobiographical tale" (*povest'*) tends toward the large "novel" (*roman*), he undoubtedly has chiefly in mind one of the most remarkable features of the *Life*—its brilliant and lifelike characterization. There are scores of characters in the work, and some are barely sketched, while others emerge as full-length portraits. The central figure—the Archpriest himself—is of course the most vivid, again largely through contrast. Now he is the fiery preacher, exhorting his flock not to give up the old ways; now he is the tender father, who writes of how his little son Ivan, during the stay in Siberia, "stole away from home that he might dwell with me; and Pashkov ordered him to be flung into the freezing dungeon where I lay; dear little lad, he spent the night there and was nigh frozen to death!" Now he thunders at the assembled clergy at the church council of 1667 and defends the old orthodoxy with learned quotation from patristic literature, and now writes of his inveterate tormentor Pashkov: "For ten years he had tormented me, or I him— I know not which. God will decide on the Day of Judgment." Strangely, this fanatic also has a sense of humor; he writes with evident amusement, as well as compassion, of an incident in the long journey to Siberia, when his devoted wife, Nastasya Markovna, came close to the breaking point:[23] "The country was savage, the natives warlike; to be separated from the horses we do not dare, but keep up with the horses we cannot, famished and weary as we are. The poor *protopopitsa* [archpriest's wife] plods along and plods along, and she takes a tumble—it's mighty slippery! Another time, as she was plodding along, she took a tumble, and another weary fellow was plodding after her, and he took a tumble in the same place; they both yell, and can't get up. The peasant yells: 'Mistress, little mother, forgive me!' And the *protopopitsa* yells: 'What are you doing, friend, trying to crush me!'" This has a grimly funny look, like some slapstick popular comedy. Then comes the swift contrast. "I come up; and she complains to me, poor woman, saying: 'Will these torments last long, archpriest?' And I said: 'Markovna, until our death.' She sighed, and answered: 'All right, Petrovich. So let's get going.'"

Next to her husband this indomitable woman is the vividest figure in the *Life*. It is she who saves the children when the raft sinks; she endures the harsh journey along Lake Irgen; she keeps up the spirits of her fainting sons. And when even the iron

71

archpriest himself falters momentarily in his resolution, thinking of what his obduracy is costing his wife and children, it is Nastasya Markovna who says to him: "The Lord have mercy! What are you saying, Petrovich? The children and I bless you: be bold to preach the word of God, and have no concern about us. . . . Go, go into the church, Petrovich, unmask their heretical whoredom!"[24]

Here, then, for certainly the first time in Russian literature, is a gallery of genuine, living people, of all conditions, from the Tsar to the poor half-wit whom Avvakum befriends. There is also, it may be added, a living landscape—the fascinating and terrible landscape of Siberia. These things are marks of a very great—and probably thoroughly unconscious—literary skill. Unhappily they remain isolated, far ahead of their times. It was perhaps Turgenev who first uttered an appreciation of the literary qualities of Avvakum's *Life*: for most of the eighteenth and nineteenth centuries it was no more than one of numerous "Old Believer" texts, a violent, fanatical, intemperate, intolerant tract. This it is, of course—but it is also an intensely human document, and written in a language that as Turgenev says, "Every writer should study without fail."

Unusual as it is, Avvakum's is not the only seventeenth century autobiography. That of another "Old Ritualist," the monk Epifany,[25] is an instructive contrast, from which one realizes most fully the altogether exceptional character of Avvakum's work. Epifany, although he suffered some persecution, did not have to undergo the long years of torment that Avvakum recounts so vividly of himself; he was, moreover, a milder and less belligerent representative of the Raskol than Avvakum. His *Life*, while factual and concrete in its details, is constructed entirely in accordance with the ordinary canon of the "saint's life," and throughout in the conventional Russo-Slavonic language. It is, moreover, as its principal Soviet investigator has called it, a "didactic autobiography," the principal substance of which is its homiletic content, introduced at points where the author's personal experiences give plausible occasion for preaching. It is thus an altogether conventional and nearly colorless work—a striking contrast with Avvakum's brilliantly, indeed luridly, colored *Autobiography*.

Autograph pages from "The Life of the Archpriest Avvakum"

Patriarch Nikon, 1672

CHAPTER III

POPULAR ORAL VERSE IN CONTACT WITH WRITTEN LITERATURE

A. Raeshnyi *and* Skomoroshnyi *Verse*

The history of Russian verse begins in the seventeenth century; medieval Russian literature, although rich in various forms of ornamented and rhythmical prose, knows no such thing as verse. That verse forms existed, however, in oral use throughout the Middle Ages is an almost certain inference from their sudden appearance in recordings made in the seventeenth and eighteenth centuries, and from various traces in prose works.

When verse does appear for the first time in Russian written literature, there are two varieties of it, of completely diverse origins, although sharing some characteristics in common, and probably interpenetrating to some extent. The first of these varieties is termed "democratic" verse by the Soviet critics, as being in its origin a native product and associated, though not exclusively, with the non-aristocratic classes of society; the second is designated "syllabic" and is associated almost exclusively with court circles. At the point of intersection as it were of these two lines is the variety known rather illogically as "pre-syllabic" verse, that is, verses with paired end-rhymes, but without fixed and uniform length of line.

There were evidently several oral or "folklore" types of verse known to the Russian Middle Ages, reflections of which first appear in the seventeenth century. Most primitive and least "poetical" is certainly the kind of jingle which is usually known as *raeshnyi* verse. This belongs to the realm of proverbs and popular sayings; the rhyme perhaps had a mnemonic value, and certainly served to emphasize and dramatize the thought. Other languages, e.g. English and German, have independently developed exactly the same kind of thing, although it has never been utilized in these languages for quasi-literary purposes. English examples would be such weather-lore as: "Red sky at morning—sailor take warning; red sky at night—sailor's delight," or "Rain before seven, clear before eleven." The Russian peasant was apparently fond of the meaningless jingle of *rzhi* (rye) and *lzhi* (lie), as seen, e.g. in the seventeenth-century "democratic" "Epistle of One Nobleman to Another": "I have a little rye, there is in me no lie." Even the nobleman Ivan Khvorostinin, whose chief literary monument is a very lengthy piece of "pre-syllabic" verse directed against heretics, is reported to have composed the "epigram": "The people of Muscovy sow the ground with rye *(rozh'iu)*, but all live with a lie *(lozh'iu)*." Sometimes a whole fairly long piece is made up of a list of personal names, each provided with a chiming adjective or noun. As investigators have noted, the *raeshnyi* verse is essentially two-membered: two parallel statements are involved, and the verbal parallelism is likely, even accidentally, to result in rhyme, especially of verb forms, when these, as is often the case, come at the end of a colon. Thus, from the same "Epistle of One Nobleman to Another,"[1] the statement: "At trials they torture *(putaiut)*, but truth they do not recognize *(znaiut)*"; "The truth I speak *(glagoliu)*, verily I do not lie *(ne lzhiu)*." From this two-membered structure with end rhymes of verb forms probably descends the standard "pre-syllabic" verse, which is always in couplets with usually verb rhymes or assonances.

By its very nature the *raeshnyi* doggerel tends toward a satirical content. When the so-called "pre-syllabic" verse system is evolved, the *raeshnyi stikh* certainly plays a large part in the process, and with it goes the connection with satire. One of the best examples of this development is the "Epistle of One Nobleman to Another" *(Poslanie dvorianina k dvorianinu)*[1] mentioned above. The "Epistle" purports to be written by a nobleman named Ivanets Funikov to some noble person who is his patron and protector, but from the style it has been very plausibly conjectured that Funikov commissioned a *skomorokh,* or popular minstrel-buffoon, to compose it in his name. The situation has historical interest; in 1606 the rebel army of Ivan Bolotnikov retreated from Moscow, and briefly held out in Tula until the forces of Tsar Vasily Shuisky overwhelmed it. Funikov's estates were among those ravaged by what he calls the "Tula brigands." The nobleman himself came off rather badly at the hands of the rebels, but has at least saved his life; his property, however, is ruined, and he appeals for assistance:

> My arms, sire, the Tula brigands
> Broke torturing me,
> And they arrayed them all over with hooks,
> And thrust me into a prison,
> And the cell, sire, was narrow
> And a great anguish seized me,
> And a rye mat was spread
> And it wasn't comfortable to sleep.
> I stayed there for thirteen weeks
> And looked out of the prison.
> And the peasants, like Poles,
> Twice summoned me to the block,
> For my old tricks
> They wanted to throw me down from the tower,
> And they torture [me] with tortures
> And do not recognize the truth.
> "Tell the truth," they say,
> "And tell no lie."
> And I swore to them
> And was knocked off my feet,
> And lay on my side.
> "I haven't much rye,
> There is in me no lie,
> Truthfully I'm speaking,
> In truth I do not lie."
> And they don't recognize this,
> And torture still more.

A little later Funikov describes his destitution in the words:

> They left me no wisp of wool
> Nor horse nor cow,
> And on the land not a handful sown;
> All told, I had my life [and] a cow,
> And she not whole;
> God sees
> She has a broken horn.

The *raeshnyi* influence can be clearly seen in such jingling lines as: *"A az im bozhilsia, i s nog svalilsia, i na bok lozhilsia: nemnogo u menia rzhi, net vo mne lzhi,"* or in the description of the petitioner's cow: *"vsego u menia zhivota korova, i ta ne zdorova; vidit Bog, slomila rog."*

The tone of the "Epistle of One Nobleman to Another" is ironic and somewhat bantering; the writer makes light of his sufferings, but he is in earnest in entreating relief.

B. *The* Bylina

Another form of oral verse, the first written records of which date from the seventeenth century, is that of the popular epic or *bylina*. This type of oral ballad (called also *starina*) has an origin that in all probability goes back to the Kievan, perhaps even the pre-Christian, period of Russian history. Since, however, it is by definition a non-written variety of verse, nothing certain can be said of its existence before the date in the seventeenth century when some partial recordings and adaptations of it appear in written form. Tsar Alexei Mikhailovich banned the performance of the oral ballads, on the grounds of their often anti-governmental content, and from the eighteenth century they were preserved chiefly in two peripheral areas: the Cossack regions of the southeast and the far northern regions of the northeast, and in Siberia. Nineteenth-century amateurs took down the *byliny* from the oral performances of popular singers, and large variorum editions of these exist. Soviet scholars have contrived a rather artificial collective edition (of N.V. Vodovozov), bringing all the known ballads loosely into two "cycles," which the editor calls respectively *Slovo o stol'nom Kieve i russkikh bogatyriakh*, in seven cantos, and *Gospodin velikii Novgorod*, in three cantos ("Tale of the Capital Kiev and the Russian Bogatyrs," and "Lord Novgorod the Great").[2] The ballads, however, do not really form anything like an "epic," but can be compared in content and interrelations with the—largely prose—English compositions about King Arthur, and the French "Carolingian cycle." The focus of the first "cycle" is the court of a prince of Kiev named Vladimir, behind whom may be made out shadowy reminiscences of two historical figures of that name, Vladimir Svyatoslavovich "the Saint" (973-1015) and Vladimir Monomakh (1113-1125). The royal figure, like King Arthur and King Charlemagne, has a character of the most contradictory kind, entirely in keeping with his composite origins: now he is a kind, hospitable, noble and valiant monarch, and now a capricious and suspicious tyrant, susceptible to the wiles of slanderers and craven in the face of danger. Around him are gathered a group of "bogatyrs," mighty men of valor—Ilya Muromets, Alyosha Popovich, Mikhailo Potok, etc.—whose exploits against Russia's foes form the chief substance of the ballads. These foes, like the person of Russia's prince, vary confusingly. It may be assumed that in the earliest versions these would have been the people of the steppe—Pechenegs and Polovtsy—against whom the princes of the Kievan federation fought historically. With them were confused in later times the Tatars, who tyrannized all Russia from the middle of the thirteenth century to the end of the sixteenth. Ivan the Terrible destroyed the Khanates of Kazan and Astrakhan early in his reign (1552-1556), and this event effectively marked the end of the Tatar menace, although the khans of the Crimea continued to raid the country until the reign of Catherine the Great. Since the Tatars, in their later period, were Muslim, the theme of the defense of Holy Russia against the infidels is prominent in the *byliny*.

Efforts of modern scholars to extract actual historical references from the *byliny* are entirely fallacious and misguided. In the course of centuries of oral transmission whatever historical kernel any incident may have had has been inevitably made unrecognizable by the accretions of later stages. What is historical about the *byliny* is the general ethos of the medieval Russian people, and particularly its patriotism, optimism in spite of adversity and oppression, its devotion to faith and family, and even its humor.

The *byliny*, as recorded in the nineteenth-century collections, are composed in an irregular verse form which eighteenth-century imitators (e.g. Karamzin) tried to regularize as "trochaic-dactylic" verse—that is, essentially, as three trochees followed by a dactyl, and unrhymed. Such a regular line does not often occur in the ballads, although lines of four accents are the commonest, and the dactylic ending is a prevalent one. There is no standard *bylina* line; it cannot even be said that the movement of the line is normally trochaic. The number of accents varies frequently from three to six, and if a bookish prosodic system were to be imposed, one would have to say that all varieties of "feet" find place in it.

It is generally agreed among scholars that the sixteenth century, with the spectacular victories of Ivan IV over the Tatars of Kazan and Astrakhan, ushered in a new age in the history of Russian oral epic. "Historical songs," which attempt to catch the significance of actual historical events, make their first appearance at that time; and the old *byliny*, newly adapted to the changed conditions of the centralized Muscovite tsardom, become current once more. At the same time it appears that the influence of the western "chivalric tale" also begins to make itself felt in the same circles in which the national epos was at home, with a result which may be seen in the "Story of the Kiev Bogatyrs," a literary reworking of the oral tradition combined with elements completely foreign to it. In this connection it is well to bear in mind that the concept of "popular oral literature" does not at all imply that the audience of such compositions was necessarily one of commoners. In an age when knowledge of reading and writing could be presupposed for only the clerical portion of the population, and even a nobleman might be, if not illiterate, at least insufficiently skilled to find reading an enjoyment, oral composition was a universal literary language, accessible to boyar and muzhik alike. It is only with the rapid progress of literacy, especially among the merchant class of the bigger cities, that a class differentiation begins, and oral poetry and its professional performers descend to the "lower classes," while the "upper classes" busy themselves with the production and enjoyment of a new "bookish" literature. Since it is the merchant class of the cities which chiefly delights in the western "chivalric tale," of the type of "Bova Korolevich" and "Uruslan Lazarevich," it is not surprising that elements of this kind of entertainment literature, especially the erotic element, find their way into the original heroic *byliny*, just as elements of the *bylina* style—the constant epithet, the negative comparison, the technique of retardation, etc., find their way, as we have seen, into the chivalric prose tales.

From the seventeenth century come three recordings of *byliny*,[3] which are, as has been mentioned, the oldest such recordings in existence. They are "Alyosha and Tugarin Zmeevich," describing the exploit of Alyosha Popovich in freeing Kiev from a foreign (Muslim) tyrant who has seized the power with the facile consent of Prince Vladimir; and two tales of love and adventure, "Mikhail Potok" and "Ivan Godinovich." "Mikhail Potok" is particularly close to the translated chivalric tale, and constructed in such a way as to arouse the reader's (or hearer's) interest by complication of plot, the folk-tale technique of threefold repetition of a situation, each time heightened, and the like. It is quite far from the primitive tale of a bogatyr's heroic exploits in defense of his country and his faith, and it reflects the growing seventeenth-century taste for literature of pure entertainment.

Presumably the *bylina* recordings which we have from the seventeenth century are more or less accurate transcripts from the oral repertory of some singer. They are not, however, "tape recordings," and much is lost. Intended for reading and not reciting, they drop the repetitions which are such a noticeable feature of oral poetry; the verse is not always accurately reproduced and there are prosy interpolations, sometimes intended to present the heroic bogatyrs in a religious light as conventionally pious. But even with these lapses from accuracy, they are still recognizably *byliny*. The situation is different when we come to the "Tale of the Kiev Bogatyrs," also of the seventeenth century. Here some anonymous author, almost certainly a townsman and probably of the merchant class, has deliberately thrown together two *bylina* plots, that about Ilya Muromets and the pagan Idolishche, and that about Alyosha Popovich and Tugarin Zmeevich. The conflation is done quite skillfully, preserving the chief features of the *bylina* style. What stands out rather grotesquely is the anachronism which introduces the manners, ceremonial, even in part the language of the seventeenth-century Muscovite court into the court of eleventh-century Kiev!

C. Lyric Verse: The Richard James and Kvashnin Collections

Among the most primitive varieties of verse in most literatures is the lyric, the outpourings of the singer's feelings, whether communal, as in the seasonal songs celebrating the return of spring, or personal—lamentations, love songs, and the like. Such a lyric literature can only be guessed at in the case of the eastern Slavs; it is very probable that it existed, but until the seventeenth century only shadowy and indirect evidence for it is to be found. In that century several small collections of verse make their appearance, the nature of which has been disputed, but which certainly indicate the existence of popular lyric and the beginnings of its assimilation with bookish literature.

In 1619-20 an English visitor named Richard James, an Oxford graduate, spent some time in Moscow and Kholmogory in the far north. When he returned to England he took with him a copy of six anonymous songs which he had induced some Russian to write out for him in a more or less phonetic English script. The manuscript is now in the Bodleian Library, and is the earliest extant example of Russian song.[4] The six pieces are, however, by no means "popular"; they were unquestionably composed by literate people, but make use in some cases of popular devices. One, describing the return of the Patriarch Filaret, father of Tsar Mikhail Romanov, from Polish exile (1619), borrows some of the very phraseology of the Tsar's announcement of the event, and belongs obviously to court circles. Another, which celebrates the retreat of the Crimean Tatar Khan Kazi-Girei from Moscow in 1598, seems to echo the official position of the Russian church toward that event, which considered it a miraculous intervention of God and the saints which protected the Russian capital. The song begins in the popular style, reminiscent of the "negative comparisons" in the *Song of Igor's Campaign*:

> Not a mighty cloud has covered the sky,
> Nor mighty thunders have thundered;
> Whither travels the dog, the Crimean tsar?
> To the mighty tsardom of Muscovy.

A very interesting piece in the James collection is the song about "spring service." It is put in the mouths of the young gentlemen of the service gentry who pray God that He may grant them "spring service" for the Tsar, and not send them on the irksome "winter service." The miseries of this are described at the beginning of the poem, in one of the five-line stanzas into which it is divided: "The shore quakes, the sand is scattered ("berezhochik *zybletsia,* da pesochik *sypletsia*"), the ice breaks, the good horses drown, the young fellows pine away." The song ends with a description of "spring service," quite close in style to popular lyric. Nonetheless it is apparent that the piece was composed in an urban milieu and for an urban clientele—the service gentry—and not by the "people."

Three of the songs from the James collection are lamentations, again in popular style, but evidently of urban origin. One mourns the sudden death, suspected to be by poison, of Prince Mikhail Skopin-Shuisky:[5]

> Now what has happened with us in Moscow—
> from midnight they have been ringing our bells.
> But the Muscovite merchants burst into tears:
> —"Now we have bowed down our heads,
> because our general is no more,
> Prince Mikhailo Vasilevich! . . ."

The prominence given in this song to the "Moscow merchants," who are the first to mourn Skopin-Shuisky's untimely death, is evidence that the piece was composed by a townsman, himself perhaps a merchant.

A second lamentation, and from a literary standpoint the most successful poem from the collection, is put in the mouth of Xenia Godunova, the hapless daughter of Boris Godunov, who was first ravished by the Pretender, and then relegated to a distant convent:[6]

A little bird is singing herself a dirge,
a little white quail.
—Alack, I must sorrow, so young—
They would burn the fresh oak-tree,
destroy my little nest,
kill my little ones,
catch me, the little quail.
A princess in Moscow is singing herself a dirge,
—Alack, I must sorrow, so young,
because a traitor is riding to Moscow,
the renegade Grishka Otrepev,
because he wants to take me captive,
and when he has taken me, to cut my hair,
to make me of a nun's estate.
But I have no mind to be shorn,
nor to keep a nun's estate:
the dark cell will open,
to gaze at the fine young men.
But alack, our dear halls,
who shall walk along you,
after our royal way of life,
and after Boris Godunov? . . .

The metaphor of the maiden as a bird is a familiar one in Russian folklore, from which it was imported into this song.

Another small collection of seventeenth-century lyric was discovered and published by M.N. Speransky (1932). They are written on records of the Kvashnin-Samarin family, and date to about 1681. Their discoverer believed that he had found a cache of genuine popular songs which Peter Andreevich Kvashnin, in whose hand they are, had transcribed from an oral source. It has since, however, been conclusively proved by V.V. Danilov that the songs were composed by Kvashnin, not transcribed. The texts are filled with revisions, lines and words crossed out, unfinished words, and the like; and however similar the themes may be to those known from later eighteenth-century collections of popular song, there is no instance of real verbal correspondence. Danilov's conclusion is that we have to do with "the author's rough draft." Another scholar, L.S. Sheptaev, calls Kvashnin: "A nobleman poet of the seventeenth century, who, in distinction to the moralizing and sermonizing poetry of his contemporary S[imeon] Polotsky, composed verses of love and ordinary life, and relied in so doing not on virshi, but on the traditions of popular song."[7]

One noteworthy feature of the collection is the repetitiveness of theme. Most of the songs are concerned with a situation in which an abandoned lover laments the absence or faithlessness of a partner. In most cases the abandoned one is a girl, but occasionally a boy. The circumstances of separation are referred to only vaguely; as in Provençal medieval lyric, it sometimes appears that malicious slanderers (the Provençal *lauzengiers*) have brought about an estrangement. The abandoned one sometimes pledges a hopeless love until death, sometimes threatens to find solace with another lover. The poems are filled with clichés, repeated monotonously from one to another, and the language is often hyperbolical. The stylistic devices, images, symbols, etc., of popular song are often employed. Thus, for example, one of the songs begins with the popular "negative comparison":

> It is not a she-dove cooing with the he-dove—
> It is a sister [i.e., mistress] speaking with a brother [i.e., lover] .[8]

In another the swan takes the place of the dove in metaphoric guise:[9]

> On a quiet cove a white she-swan cried out
> In a loud voice, very piteously,
> And lamented over the white he-swan
> Because the white he-swan had abandoned her,
> "My white he-swan has taken up with another she-swan."

The metaphor is then dropped, as in the song about Xenia Godunova, and the human situation is described:

> In the lofty *terem* a fair maiden sits under the window,
> Her bright eyes are tear-swollen.

At this point two lines have been inserted in the manuscript between two already written—clear evidence of an author's "rough draft" rather than of a transcript from an oral performance:

> In tears she pronounces words,
> Vehemently she spoke words.

85

Presently the omnipresent bird-metaphor appears once more in the girl's lamentation:

> Ah, it was not a peacock walking in the court,
> It did not drop a golden feather:
> A fair maiden was walking on the clear plain.*
> She gazed at the precious, precious red gold,
> More precious than the clean, even-sloping [rounded?] pearl,
> More precious than this is my dear one, my darling.

[*"on the clear plain"—*vo chisto polia*—a cliché from the popular ballad literature, but here ungrammatical—literally, "on clear (singular) plains (plural)."]

There is another, rather similar, small collection of songs, of about the same date, from the archive of the Kostroma nobleman S.I. Pazukhin. According to the conjecture of their discoverer, these songs were composed by Pazukhin when he, at the age of 30, was sent on a service expedition by the Tsar and found himself separated from his wife and family. The popular songs of separation thus appealed by their content to him, and he composed imitations of them, as in all likelihood Kvashnin had also done.

The closeness of all these collections of what are quite certainly the work of literate urban writers to the style of popular verse is apparent not only in the images, stylistic devices and the like, but even in the verse form. One poem from the James collection is composed in 5-line strophes, but the rest of the poems in all these collections are in unrhymed lines of irregular length and number of accents, very much like the *bylina* line. There is no evidence of familiarity with the bookish syllabic system of verse composition.

D. The "Tale of Sorrow and Misfortune" ("Povest' o Gore i Zlochastii")

Certainly the most remarkable monument of the seventeenth-century amalgamation of the popular and the literate is the verse "Tale," found in a single manuscript, entitled "Tale of Sorrow and Misfortune: How Sorrow-Misfortune Brought a Young Man to the Monkish Estate."[10] In this anonymous piece we find a quite extraordinary mélange of genres, such as genuinely popular composition never tolerates. The verse form, like that of the imitative lyrics, is very close to *bylina* verse, and so are many of the devices—e.g. standard epithets, such as "green wine," "white body," "gray wolf," "bright eyes," etc.; the use of double words, e.g. "Sorrow-Misfortune" *(Gore-Zlochastie)* itself, "to steal-rob," "drunk-merry," "feed-eat," "family-tribe," etc.; the repetition of words, especially prepositions, etc. Even the situations and their descriptions are reminiscent of the *byliny*, e.g. the young man's polite conduct on entering a banquet hall, etc. But the piece is not a *bylina*: the hero is no *bogatyr* and the action is not heroic but commonplace; the milieu is that of the merchant class. There is also a distinct lyric element, seen most notably in the young man's "little song" on the bank of the river, when he realizes that he has nothing more to lose and may as well be cheerful. Still more distinct, and this time quite alien to the quasi-popular character of the rest of the "Tale" is the didactic, religious element. The unknown author begins his piece with a pious invocation: "By the will of our Lord God and Savior, Jesus Christ Almighty, from the beginning of the age of man!" He then launches into a page summarizing the Genesis account of the origin of sin, with the interesting (and for his story, appropriate) variant that the "forbidden fruit" is "the fruit of the vine." Adam and Eve's transgression angers God, who "plunged them into great calamity, struck them with great sorrow and boundless ignominious disgrace, evil penury, enemy invasions, evil, immeasureable nakedness and shoelessness, infinite wretchedness, and extreme want, thus making us humble and bringing us on the way of salvation." The hyperbolical emphasis on the physical destitution of our first parents when they had angered God, which the Biblical account scarcely hints at, is in harmony with the author's picture of Gore-Zlochastie as "naked and shoeless, without a stitch on it," when it first appears to the young man, and the general atmosphere that seems to equate happiness with affluence and "Sorrow-Misfortune" with poverty.

The "Tale" itself begins with the introduction of a nameless "young man" (molodets) whose mother and father instruct him in the traditional moral conduct of old Muscovy:

> Don't go, child, to banquets and to picnics [bratchiny],
> Do not sit in the best place,
> Do not drink, child, two cups after one!
> Furthermore, child, do not give your eyes freedom,
> Do not be led astray, child, toward well-born, beautiful wives—
> The daughters of [noble?] fathers," etc.

The young man, however, "was at that time young and foolish," and "wished to live as he pleased" (a khotel zhiti, kak emu liubo). His first experience is flattering: "He earned fifty rubles, and he acquired for himself fifty friends" (nazhival molodets piat'desiat' rublyov, zalez on sebe piat'desiat' druzhov). One of the fifty entices the young man to drink the "green" (i.e., "new") wine until he falls asleep, promising to watch over him. When he awakes, the youth finds his money and clothes—and the solicitous friend—gone. The young man soliloquizes:

> God gave me a great livelihood—
> [now] there is nothing to eat-devour!
> When money is no more, not even half-money,—
> Then friend is no more, not even half-friend:
> Family and clan deny [one] (rod i plemia otchitaiutsia)
> All friends renounce [one] (vse druzi proch' otpiraiutsia)

Humbled and ashamed to return to father and mother the young man goes to a "foreign land," and some hospitable people invite him to share a banquet with them. He behaves with exemplary courtesy: "He bowed down to the miraculous ikons, he bent his head to the gentlefolk in all four directions"; but amid the festivities "the young man sits cheerless, miserable, sorrowful, joyless." His hosts inquire the reason, and when he tells his story, they counsel him to behave modestly and circumspectly in a foreign land, and he will again win fortune and friends. He follows their advice and soon is on his feet once more. At this point he makes the fatal mistake of bragging:

> "I have earned—I, the young man—
> A greater living than my old one!"
> Sorrow-Misfortune heard
> The young man's boasting,
> And spoke itself such a word:
> "Don't brag, young man, of your fortune,
> Don't boast of your wealth.
> I, Sorrow, have had people
> Both wiser and cleverer than you,
> And I, Sorrow, have outwitted them;
> Great misfortune has commenced for them."

This is the first appearance in the "Tale" of the sinister character which gives it its name. Sorrow-Misfortune (*Gore-Zlochastie*) is a personification of a somewhat enigmatic sort. It (both names are neuter, but the figure is thought of in a male human guise) is at once an external "fate" and a kind of double of the young man himself, whose desire to "live as he pleases" and not be bound by the safe, conventional rules of conduct, defines and determines this fate. After the first appearance of Sorrow-Misfortune, brought on by the young man's boasting, Gore appears to him in a dream and tempts him to abandon his safe, philistine existence and lose his wealth and respectability in the tavern. In spite of the dream intervention of the Archangel Gabriel, who warns him not to listen, this is what happens: the young man drinks away his money and fine clothes. He then flees until he comes to a river which he cannot cross because he has no money to pay the ferryman. Hungry and despairing, he soliloquizes lyrically:

> Woe is me, sorrowful Misfortune!
> It has brought me, young man, to poverty:
> It has slain me, young man, with deadly hunger,
> Three days have already been joyless for me;
> I, young man, have not eaten even a half-bite of bread!
> But I, young man, shall throw myself into the swift river—
> Wash my body, swift river,
> And fishes, eat my white body,—
> That is better for me than this despised life.
> Shall I escape from the Sorrow of misfortune?

One might suppose that suicide in despair would be precisely the outcome which Sorrow-Misfortune, as an independent, external malignity, might desire for its victim. But there is another side to this complex personification, which is indicated in the title of the "Tale": "How Sorrow-Misfortune brought a young man to the monkish estate." Nothing indicates that the salvation of the young man's soul is the conscious purpose of Gore; perhaps Sorrow-Misfortune is, like Goethe's Mephistopheles, the impotent tool of the Almighty, that "always wills evil, and always works good" (*die stets bas Böse will, und stets das Gute schafft*). It should be noted that in his paraphrase of the Genesis account of the sin of Adam and Eve, the author stresses that their punishment was "to make us humble and bring us to salvation." In any case, Gore's program, whatever divine purpose it may ultimately serve, is to drive the young man to the utter limit of misery, and suicide, with fish eating his "white body," disagreeable as it may be, is not this utter limit.

Hitherto Sorrow-Misfortune has not revealed itself to its victim directly; first it soliloquizes unseen, when the young man's untimely boast evokes it (Herodotus would probably have spoken here of "envy of the gods"; the Russian writer merely quotes the proverb: "boasting is rotten"). Then Gore insinuates itself into the young man's dream, with its temptations. Now, as the youth is on the point of throwing himself into the river,

> At that hour by the swift river
> Sorrow leaped from behind a stone,
> Barefoot-naked, Sorrow had not a stitch on,
> Yet Sorrow was girt with a bast thong,
> [And] it shouted in a bogatyr voice:
> "Stop, young man!
> You are not going to escape me, Sorrow, anywhere;
> Don't cast yourself into the swift river,
> And don't keep grieving in sorrow—
> But live in sorrow,
> Be ungrieving,
> And abandon grief in sorrow."

The sense of this curious admonition seems to be: "When you are entirely destitute, as you are now, you have nothing more to lose, and so you should be cheerful and gay." The young man understands the words so, and sings a "little song," which is the chief lyric portion of the "Tale"; and pointedly the author calls the song: *khoroshuiu napevochku ot velikogo krepkogo razuma*— "a fine little song from a great powerful intelligence":

> My mother bore me free of sorrow.
> With a little comb she combed my curls,
> she dressed me in expensive garments
> and stepping back, shading her eyes with her hand, she inspected me:
> "Does my child look well in expensive garments?
> Why, in expensive garments my child is beyond price."
> How she would prophesy this way before I grew up!
> And I myself know this and realize it,
> that there's putting together of a scarlet cloak without a master,
> no comforting a child without its mother,
> no being rich for a drunkard,
> no being in good repute for a dicer.
> I was enjoined in my parents' house
> that I should be as white as snow,
> but that I was born a fire-brand. [11]

The little song attracts the ferrymen, who carry the youth across the river for nothing and give him food, drink, and clothes. But Sorrow is not done with him; it now pursues him in various animal guises; the episode reflects both the heroic *byliny* and the popular *skazka* ("fairy tale"), in which pursuit often takes such a form:

> When the young man is on the clear plain [*na chistom pole*],
> Malevolent Sorrow has gone ahead.
> On the clear plain it met the young man,
> began to caw over the young man,
> Like a malevolent raven over a falcon.
> . . . .
> The young man took wing, a bright falcon,
> But Sorrow after him, a white gyrfalcon;
> The young man took wing, a steel-blue dove,
> But Sorrow after him, a gray hawk;
> The young man began to run on the plain, a gray wolf,
> But Sorrow after him with swift greyhounds;
> The young man became on the field feather-grass,
> But Sorrow came on with a keen scythe."

The denouement comes very rapidly. The last degree of "sorrow-misfortune," to which the young man might be driven, would be a life of crime and the loss of his immortal soul. So Gore "instructs the young man to live richly, to kill and rob—so that they may hang the young man for this, or put him in the water with a stone." It is here that the victim rebels, and flees into a monastery —"but Sorrow stops at the holy gates, clings to the young man no more."

Here we may again ponder the author's meaning. Gore-Zlochastie is the personification of man's ill-fate that hounds him through his whole life. But it is not a merely external force, it is in a sense the victim's own creation. It would doubtless be carrying the point too far to suggest that the young hero of the "Tale" has something in common with Dostoevsky's "Underground Man,"—but both are clearly the creators of their own misery, and with both their own "sweet will" is the supreme value. The young man rejects the comfortable, conventional life of his class to "live as he pleases"—and this brings about his first misfortune, the tavern robbery. But note: this one misfortune is not a part of the relentless persecution of Gore-Zlochastie. It is only when he boasts of his success *in spite of* misfortune that Gore begins to pursue him. When, yielding to the seductive dream in spite of the Archangel's warning, he forsakes his bride and his respectable middle class life, and deliberately chooses to spend his substance in riotous living—that Gore has him in its power. Like the Underground Man, he has chosen a *free* life, with misery, rather than an unfree one, with affluence. The outcome of the two tales is of course different: worn down by Gore's persecution, the young man at last balks at conduct which would lose him not only his life, but his soul—though the author does not expressly say so—and takes the only course left to him, which is the renunciation of the freedom that has cost him so much, and submission once more to the strictest of corporate control of his fate, that of the monastery.

The "Tale of Sorrow-Misfortune" is philosophically the most profound work of Russian seventeenth-century literature. It is also one of the most artistic. For the first time the fate of a man is depicted as his own work; and it is a common man, not a prince or a saint, but a young merchant. The author's purpose is still didactic:

he wants, by a terrible example, to deter others from abandoning the precepts of father and mother and living "as they please." But the moral is left to be inferred from the outcome of the story itself, and not tediously hammered home as Simeon Polotsky, for example, would do. Indeed, there is very little auctorial comment in the story, and most of the development is put in the form of direct speech, and is thus objective.

The "characterization" is primitive. The young man is sketched with somewhat contradictory traits, but there is no attempt at rounding out his personality; he is a mere puppet. And "Sorrow-Misfortune" can hardly be a real person, since allegory by its very nature of typization is a denial of the personal element.

Mention has been made of the number and importance of the popular traits in the "Tale of Sorrow-Misfortune." The author, who must certainly have been, like the anonymous hero, a member of the city merchant class, was well versed in the stylistics of the popular epic. The verse form shows this, but as some of the above-quoted lines make clear, there is a degree of rhyming in this work which the *bylina* does not know. The tendency of Russian syntax of this period to relegate verbs to the ends of cola almost necessarily results in rhyming, as for example: *ino zlo to Gore izlukavilos', vo sne molodtsa prividelos'* ("but that malevolent Sorrow devised cunningly, appeared to the young man in a dream"). Verbal rhyme is so inevitable as to be probably often unconscious; but such a rhyme as that, quoted above, of the "fifty rubles *(piat'desiat' rublyov)* and "fifty friends" *(piat'desiat' druzhov)* is certainly deliberate. We have here a device which we shall see more of in the "learned poetry" of the seventeenth century, to which we must next turn.

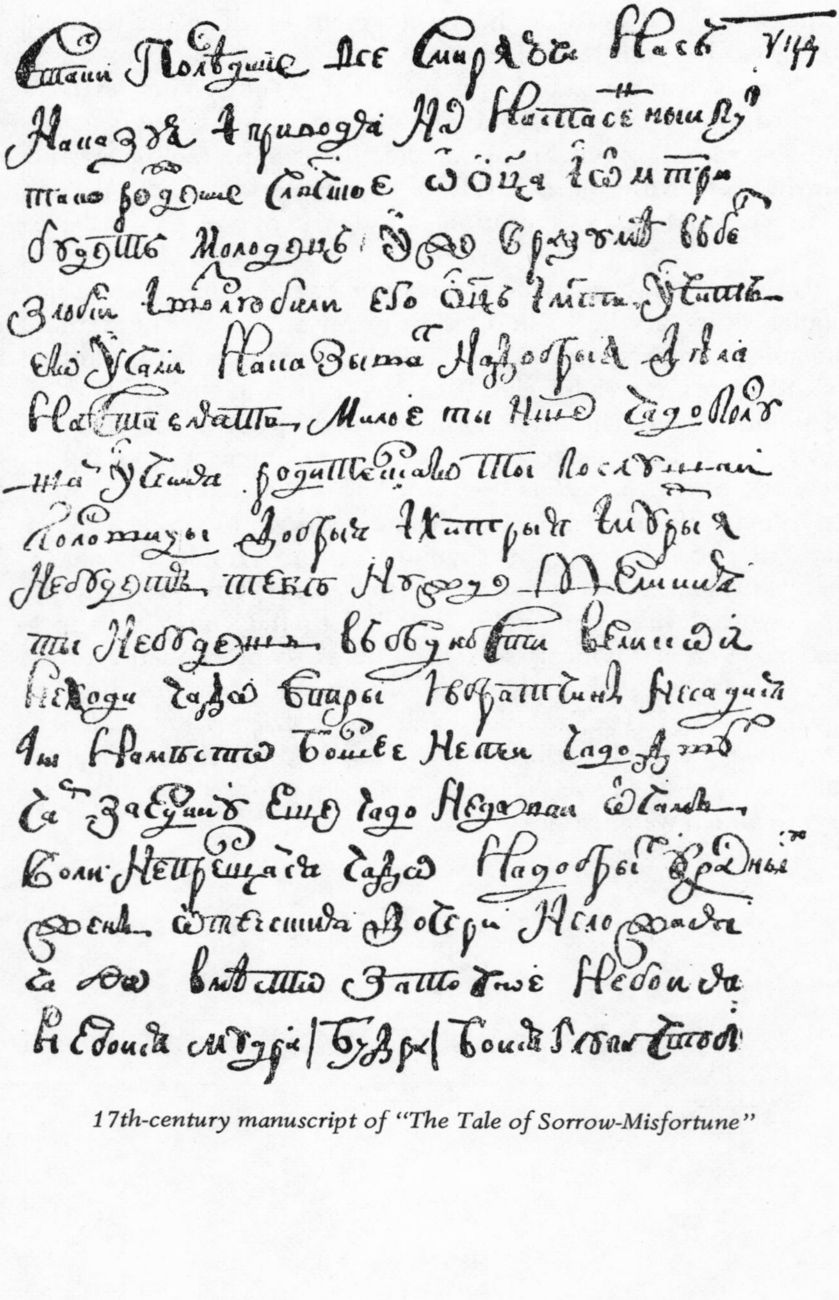

17th-century manuscript of "The Tale of Sorrow-Misfortune"

The Bible in Pictures, Vasily Koren, 1696
Adam and Eve

From the Alphabet Book of Karion Istomin, Moscow 1694.

CHAPTER IV

LEARNED OR BOOKISH POETRY IN THE SEVENTEENTH CENTURY

A. The Nature and Origins of "Syllabic" Verse

The several varieties of "democratic" verse which we have been considering hitherto—narrative, lyrical, satirical, and the unique synthesis achieved by the "Tale of Sorrow-Misfortune"—are all reflections in a written or literate form of originally oral, popular, genres. But these varieties, however interesting to a modern scholar, would in all probability have passed unnoticed in their own time. Verse as the literate public of the seventeenth century knew it is a quite different phenomenon, some account of which must now be given.

Theorists are not united in defining what features distinguish verse in general from prose; but for the older literary periods at least it may be said that recognized verse forms have in common the element of *regularity*, predictability. Thus the classical languages employ *quantitative* alternation, that is, predictable repetitions of combinations of long and short syllables. The Teutonic languages, in which "quantity" was never a meaningful element of language, created verse by the use of what is sometimes called *Stabreim*, i.e., regular repetitions of the same consonant or of a vowel at the beginnings of the words placed at predictable positions in the line. Hebrew poetry, e.g. the Psalms, makes use of *parallelism*, that is, of verses similar in length and word position, of which the second echoes the first in content.

In the classical languages each *line* of verse is measured by quantitative *feet*; there will not necessarily be identity in the

97

number of *syllables* in each line, since a foot is composed of several syllables, and different feet (e.g. dactyl and spondee) may be metrically interchangeable but with differing (e.g. two or three) numbers of syllables. In the Teutonic languages the line is measured by the number of *accents* (that is, it is *tonic*), and again the number of unaccented syllables will vary from line to line. In the Romance languages, which have all lost the quantitative element of the parent Latin, a line of verse is measured by the *number of syllables* it contains; thus we speak of *octosyllabic* Spanish verse, of the Italian *hendecasyllable* (11-syllable line), etc. With the exception of French, which has no word accent, the Romance verse forms also take cognizance of tone, and hence are qualified as *syllabo-tonic*.

In any language a line of verse is of course a *sound* unit (the notion of verse *read silently* is a very modern development, completely alien to all cultures before at least the eighteenth century). In order to mark more clearly than would otherwise be possible the *end* of a line, the Romance languages (medieval Latin, French, Provençal and Italian) developed the device of rhyme or assonance. By this device the final word of a line was made to conform in sound, either completely (true rhyme) or partially (assonance) with other line ends either directly contiguous or placed at predictable distances from each other. In the French language, which lost its original word accent during the medieval period and therefore had to rely entirely on the number of syllables to define a line—a criterion not readily apprehended by the ear—the device of rhyme came to be an obligatory element from at least the twelfth century; unrhymed French verse is still an exception, and felt as anomalous. The commonest French line, the so-called Alexandrine, employed exclusively in verse drama and very extensively in other genres, is rhymed in couplets, with alternation between masculine (one-syllable) and feminine (two-syllable) rhymes. The Alexandrine line accordingly alternates in number of syllables between twelve (masculine) and thirteen (feminine).

The original Slavic parent language (proto-Slavic) had what philologists call "free accent"—that is, the (tonic) accent might fall on any syllable in a word. Accent was moreover *significant*— that is, might distinguish different case forms of the same word, e.g. Russian *ruki*, "of a hand" (genitive singular) and *rúki*, "hands" (nominative-accusative plural), or otherwise homonymous words of completely different meanings, e.g. Russian *múka*, "torment," and *muká*, "flour." This original free accent is retained by the South Slavic (Serbo-Croatian and Bulgarian) and East Slavic (Russian, Ukrainian) languages, but lost by the West Slavic (Czech and Polish). In Polish every word of more than one syllable is uniformly accented on the penult (next to last syllable), with the very minor exception of some recent borrowings.

Poland is of course a Roman Catholic country, and its cultural ties have in historic times always been with the West. Its ecclesiastical language has been (and is) Latin, and Italian and especially French influences have always been very significant in Polish literature. The first important flowering of Polish poetry came in the sixteenth century (Rej, Kochanowski, et al.) and owed a great deal in both subjects and forms to the western Renaissance. Since tonic accent in Polish is fixed, and thus meaningless, the definition of a line of verse has, as in French, to rely on the number of syllables, and is emphasized (as also in French) by the device of rhyme. Since, however, Polish word accent is uniformly on the next to the last syllable, rhyme of necessity is always feminine, and the usual French alternation between masculine and feminine rhymes is impossible.

Until the middle of the seventeenth century the western parts of the medieval "Russian lands," that is, the Ukraine and Belorussia, were parts of the united kingdom of Lithuania-Poland. Russian annexation of the left-bank Ukraine (1654) and of Kiev on the right bank brought these regions, already quite thoroughly westernized and with a dominantly Roman Catholic upper class, into close association with the Orthodox and "Old Muscovite" culture of the rest of Russian Tsardom. Among the influences that thus reached Moscow was that of Polish verse. There is no question that the so-called "syllabic" verse (that is, verse of rhyming lines of uniform syllable count), represented by such poets as the Belorussian Simeon Polotsky and the Ukrainian Stefan Yavorsky and Dimitry Rostovsky, was a creation that owed its existence chiefly to Ukrainian and Polish influence. This verse, however, is a phenomenon of the last half of the seventeenth century, and even the first part of the eighteenth (e.g. Feofan Prokopovich and Antiokh Kantemir), and dates from the time of Muscovite control of the Ukraine. The question remains about the origin and nature of the so-called "pre-syllabic" verse, which dominates the first half of the century.

"Pre-syllabic" verse—an unfortunate designation, but one too well established to be upset—is verse (virshi) with end-rhyme in couplets, but with lines of varying length by syllable count (aniso-syllabism). A good example of "pre-syllabic" verse is the effusion which closes the "Annalistic Book" usually attributed to Prince Katyryov-Rostovsky, quoted in translation above. The general effect of this kind of verse is, to a modern ear, pedestrian and ridiculous in the extreme, because of the labored and mechanical kind of rhyme, and the incongruity (exploited in his time by the late Ogden Nash in English) of the combination of rhyme with lumbering lines otherwise quite indistinguishable from prose. Where did this variety of "verse" originate, and how is it connected with the regular "syllabic" kind that followed it?

The most up to date and scholarly account of the origins of Russian verse is to be found in the preface of Professor Alexander Mikhailovich Panchenko to his edition in the *Poet's Library* series of *Russian Syllabic Poetry of the XVIIth and XVIIIth Centuries* and more fully in his book *Russian Poetic Culture of the XVIIth Century.*[1] Professor Panchenko very properly points out that the picture of medieval Russian literature as one devoid of poetry, while generally accurate, must be modified in two regards: folklore (oral) poetry existed throughout the Middle Ages—*bylina* verse, the *raeshnik*, the various kinds of lyric, etc.—as we have seen above; and that a universal literary language, with a poetical tradition, existed throughout the Middle Ages for all the southern and eastern Slavs—Serbs, Bulgarians and Russians, even the non-Slavic Rumanians. This is the ancient Church Slavonic, which is as much a universal language for Orthodox Christendom as Latin is for the Catholic West.

When in the ninth and tenth centuries the southern and eastern Slavs accepted Christianity from Byzantium, the sacred books of the faith began to be translated into the language of the converts, since, unlike the Roman church, the Orthodox did not insist on the language of the central organization. The Greek language of the Middle Ages, as it was employed in Christian poetry, differed markedly from the classical. The quantitative metrical system had given place to an accentual kind of verse, with cola of differing lengths; and although regular rhyme did not become habitual, as it did in Latin hymnography, it often makes an accidental appearance when cola end in parallel word forms. The greatest Byzantine poet of this new kind of verse is the sixth-century Romanos called "the Melodos," that is, "Song-writer." A random example of his verse will show some typical features, including two accidental rhymes:

"Ὥσπερ οὐρανοῦ ὑετὸν   ἡ γῆ ἀποδέχεται

οὕτως ἐν τῷ "Αιδη 'Αδὰμ   κρατούμενος ἔμενε σὲ

τὸν τοῦ κόσμου <u>σωτῆρα</u>   καὶ ζωῆς τὸν <u>δωτῆρα</u>...

καὶ ἔλεγε τῷ "Αιδη   Τί μέγα φρονεῖς;

μεῖνον με, μεῖνον μικρόν ------

τὸ κράτος σου <u>λυθέντα</u>   καὶ ἐμὲ <u>ἀνυψωθέντα</u>.

> [Even as the earth awaits anxiously   the rain of heaven,
> So Adam in Hades   awaited Thee in bondage,
> The world's Savior   and giver of life;
> And he said unto Hades   "Why art thou puffed up?
> Wait for me, wait a little....
> For me to be loosed from thy power   and raised on high..."] [2]

It is worth noting, incidentally, that Romanos usually "signed" his works with an acrostic of a very simple sort, consisting of the initial letters of the successive strophes of the hymn, read in sequence. The acrostic from the Hymn on the Resurrection from which the above lines are quoted reads: *ode Romanou*, "A song of Romanos."

Quite naturally the various kinds of Byzantine hymns were translated into Church Slavonic. An excellent study of one such translation is that of G.M. Prokhorov: "Toward a History of Liturgical Poetry: the Hymns and Prayers of Patriarch Philotheos Kokkinos."[3] The Slavonic translations of the hymns of Patriarch Philotheos (1353-55; 1364-76) are very close and literal, and even attempt to maintain (for singing purposes, of course) the same lengths of line as the originals. The acrostic signatures, however, are not kept, but noted; thus, for example (Prokhorov, p. 135) the Greek acrostic ΚΟΙΝ^φΑΣ ΔΕ^чΗΣΕ^λΙΣ ΧΡΙ^οΣΤΕ Σ^θΩΝ ΔΟ^εΥΛΩΝ ^οΔΕΧΟΥ^υ, where the poet's name, ΦΙΛΟΘΕΟΥ, is intertwined with a prayer, is explained thus by the Slavonic translator: "The same has an acrostic *(kraegranesie)*: 'Receive, O Christ, the common prayers of Thy slaves,' and in the verses to the Virgin, 'Of Philotheos.'"

101

Thus medieval Slavonic hymnology, translated or imitated from Byzantine originals, may well have exercised some influence on Russian pre-syllabic verse. This conjecture is almost certain in regard to the use of acrostic signatures, sometimes very elaborate, which are such a notable feature of pre-syllabic verse. There is no other source from which the Russian poets could have learned this technique but from the Byzantine hymn-writers.

Byzantine influence, however, can certainly not account for one of the most characteristic features of pre-syllabic verse, which is the obligatory couplet rhyme. The Greek may occasionally have rhyming words in end positions, probably accidentally, as the example of Romanos shows; but rhyme is never a normal feature, nor is it of the Slavonic translations. This trait in pre-syllabic verse must have another origin.

In the development of Belorussian and Ukrainian verse the influence of Polish metrics was extremely strong, and the incorporation of Belorussia and the Ukraine into Muscovy brought these developments into the Great Russian purview. Following Polish practice, west Russian poets wrote *virshi* to accompany didactic works which were published at the very end of the sixteenth century. Curiously enough, there are two varieties of such Ukrainian and Belorussian verses, the first, exemplified by some pieces of Gerasim Smotritsky (1581), written in lines of unequal numbers of syllables; and the second, exemplified by Andrei Rymsha, a Belorussian, whose dedicatory panegyric prefixed to his "Apostol" (1591) maintains isosyllabism. Both these types were followed by subsequent west Russian poets, and there is no doubt that they exerted an influence on the seventeenth-century development of bookish verse in Muscovy. There is no reason, however, to suppose that the Smotritsky type of verse, marked by anisosyllabism, was the sole, or even the determining factor in the genesis of pre-syllabic Russian verse. There is a native factor, far older and certainly more influential.

A.M. Panchenko notes, as many scholars have done, the frequent "rhyming" passages in medieval Russian prose; we have seen some of these, e.g. in Prince Katyryov-Rostovsky's "Annalistic Book," in Avraamy Palitsyn's memoirs, and elsewhere. The notion that such passages are "embryonic verse" is completely to be rejected. They are prose, and the rhymes, where they are not purely accidental, are to be regarded as rhetorical ornaments

Above: two 'skomorokhi' singing, two dancing. Below: a one-man 'skomorokh' puppet-show.

Examples of 17th-century boyar dress, influenced by the Poles. This and the two woodcuts of 'skomorokhi' on the previous page are from Adam Olearius, "Vermehrte newe Beschreibung Der Muscowitischen und Persichen Reyse" (published 1656).

analogous to the "gorgianic figures" of the Greek rhetoricians. As Professor V.N. Peretts puts the matter:

> "The general foundation . . . of rhythmic speech provided with rhyme can be considered to be the syntactical arrangement of clauses in which the predicate, or in general the most significant words from the author's point of view, are moved forward, or placed at the end of the clause. The natural delay before a new thought-proposition gave rise quite consistently to a rhythmic character of a certain kind, which we observe even in monuments of ancient Russo-Slavonic literature which are indubitably in prose. Rhyme—originally of verbs or adjectives—seems to us the result of such an arrangement of clauses, and appeared, it is thought, independently of the author's intention, as it does also in popular epic verse, which is usually unrhymed.[4]

The connection of such rhyming passages in works of prose with the *raeshnyi* verse is quite obvious. The *raek* is, in its nature, a popular form intermediate between prose and real verse: it is two-membered in structure, and employs rhyme as either a mnemonic device or for purposes of emphasis. It was a medium used chiefly by the *skomorokhi*, or popular minstrel-buffoons, and as we have seen in the case of the "Epistle of One Nobleman to Another," it could be readily adapted to a fairly lengthy piece of narrative of a satirical or humorous sort. The leap from the typically short and more or less epigrammatic *raek* to such a quite lengthy piece as the "Epistle" is a surprising one, but can hardly be doubted. The second leap is not so certain, but highly probable: from the popular oral verse ("democratic verse") written under the influence of this, to a bookish and religious milieu and to a content of a didactic and polemical kind. There can be no doubt that here the influence of Ukrainian and Belorussian models, such as those of Gerasim Smotritsky mentioned above, played a considerable part, for anisosyllabic Ukrainian or Belorussian verse was an established medium for religious exposition—and this is in general the content of the very earliest Muscovite verse of this type. Even such an "Epistle" as that of Prince Semyon Ivanovich Shakhovskoi addressed to Prince Dmitry Pozharsky[5] has an entirely theological content; and the extant pieces of Evstraty, Nasedka and Khvorostinin are either prayers or religious polemics.

B. The Writers of Pre-Syllabic Verse

The earliest writers of "pre-syllabic" verse in Russian are a rather mixed group, with little to unite them but their literary activity. The earliest seems to be the monk Evstraty, who had been a secretary *(diak)* in secular life, in the service of Tsar Vasily Shuisky, and had written a prose account in 1613 entitled: "Tale of a Certain Contention." His verse composition is a short prayer prefixed to his *Povest'*, written in what he proudly says the Romans call "serpentine verse," a kind of metrical stunt which has to be unravelled like a puzzle.[6] Needless to say, it has interest only as a curiosity. Prince Shakhovskoi's "Epistle," already mentioned, was composed by that unfortunate nobleman, presumably as a demonstration of his orthodoxy, on the occasion when he was disgraced as a result of having entered upon an uncanonical fourth marriage. Ivan Nasedka in the 1620s composed a verse polemic entitled "Statement Against the Lutherans" *(Izlozhenie na liutory)*.[7] None of this material has the slightest literary merit.

The most interesting of this group is Prince Ivan Andreevich Khvorostinin (d. 1625):[8] but personality and not literary skill constitute the interest. Khvorostinin was in his youth a favorite of the First Pretender, and a great admirer of western ways. He was accused of being a freethinker, who despised old Muscovite ways, refused to fast in Lent, did not believe in the efficacy of prayer or the resurrection of the dead, etc. Since these allegations were all made by his enemies at the trial at which he was convicted of heresy (1623), it is hard to say whether they had any basis in fact. The only thing quite certain is that the Prince was in fact a seventeenth-century "westernizer." He was relegated to a monastery, put under very strict supervision, and brought eventually to sign a confession of faith and abjure his "heresy." While in the monastery, that is, between 1623 and his death in 1625, he composed a lengthy (some 1300 verses) polemical exposition bearing the prolix title: "Prayer to Christ God: That many suffer great servitude from the malice of unreasonable tsars and rulers, and moreover from heretics and sensual [chrevougonykh] men; such is the word of the sorrowful; having an acrostic on [initial] letters: against the Roman heresy."

The first group of "pre-syllabic" versifiers has, as noted, no cohesion. During the 1630s and 1640s, however, there flourished in Moscow a numerous coterie of such writers, to which Professor A.M. Panchenko, who has investigated it exhaustively in his volume *The Russian Verse Culture of the XVIIth Century*, applies the name *Prikaznaia Shkola*, on the grounds that the members of the group seem to have been predominantly in the service of the "departments" *(prikazy)* of the central government. It would perhaps not be too wide of the mark to call them in English the "bureaucrat school."[9] They were, however, not bureaucrats of the ordinary kind. The central focus of their activity was the *Pechatnyi Dvor*, or "Government Printing Office," and many of them, e.g. Savvaty, were *spravchiki* (literally, "correctors"), that is, editors of books to be published. Since almost all books published in Russia before the age of Peter the Great were religious, these *spravchiki* were recruited from among the intelligentsia of the monasteries. They were, as Panchenko remarks, "the intellectual élite" of the age.

Their verse takes the form chiefly of "epistles," directed to one another, to influential court personages, even on occasions to the Tsar himself. These epistles are regularly "signed" with acrostics, often very elaborate; sometimes the addressee is also noted in the acrostic. Since "intellectual subtlety" *(ostroumie)* was one of their most highly regarded values, they very frequently make parade of this by designating themselves or their addressees by riddling allusions rather than their real names: thus a person named Fyodor (Greek Theo-doros) might be indicated as "he whose name means 'gift of God'"; or the name Mikhail referred to as "he who has the name 'face of God.'" Savvaty's "intellectual subtlety" did not apparently include a knowledge of Hebrew, for "Michael" actually means: "Who is like God?"

A number of interesting and industrious writers of this "school" are enumerated by Professor Panchenko: the *spravchik*

Savvaty, Mikhail Zlobin, Peter Samsonov, etc. One of the fascinating stories of Professor Panchenko's research has to do with the nobleman Alexei Savvich Romanchukov, a high government official *(diak)* who went on a diplomatic mission for Tsar Alexei as ambassador to Persia. On the long overland journey the Russian delegation traveled part of the time in company with a German ambassadorial group, among whom were a Doctor Hartmann Gramman, and the famous Adam Olearius. Among Doctor Gramman's papers is an album, on one page of which the young Russian ambassador, with whom the doctor had become very friendly, wrote a "poem," in pre-syllabic verse, as a remembrance. Olearius's Latin account of the journey contains a description of Romanchukov and his friendship with the Germans, his eagerness to learn Latin, and so on. As Professor Panchenko remarks, this is the first Russian piece of "learned" verse to come to the attention of the western world. The story has a tragic sequel, for Romanchukov, on his return, was threatened with disgrace because of the relative lack of success of his mission, and poisoned himself. A piece of verse attributed to him and found in a kind of manuscript anthology (unpublished) may have been written while he was contemplating his action:[10]

> But I am being driven out of this world;
> My days are being taken away and my years brought to an end;
> The Jericho walls of my life are breached,
> The noises of the sounding trumpets on the marketplace are approaching.
> Moreover also two grinders are passing away,
> And friends and sincere ones are going afar,
> For the mourners on the marketplace are dispersing,
> And the queen is being led away from her place as a captive.

The imagery of this elegy is obscure, but the phrase *dva meliushchiia prestavaiut* suggests to this writer a verse of Ecclesiastes (XII, 3: *i perestanut molot' meliushchie*): "And the grinders shall cease grinding." Perhaps the connection is not entirely illusory.

The numerous poets whose professional lives were in one way or another connected with the government bureaus of the Muscovite Tsardom can, as Professor Panchenko maintains, be considered a "school" in the proper sense of the word, and not "a casual and amorphous group." The marks which define such a school Panchenko summarizes as follows:[11]

Personal and literary contacts, regularity of versifying activity, a corporate self-consciousness, formulated terminologically in the combinations "spiritual union," and then a "flowery" language, opposed to the ordinary language used in speech or practical written communication, and which demands of each author a peculiar gift and art, an "intellectual keenness."

The poets of this school practiced their art principally in the genre of the verse epistle, and one of the chief evidences of "intellectual keenness" which they exhibited was the elaborate acrostic. The preoccupation with the latter resulted all too often in "padding" with lines of fatuous irrelevance inserted only because they possessed the necessary initial letter. Such lines were even provided for the lazy by a work called the *Kraestrochnyi alfavit*, or "Acrostic Alphabet." Under such a "poetical system" mere verbalizing substituted for originality, and the essentially unpoetical character of the *virshi*, which anisosyllabism insured, was heightened to grotesqueness. No breath of genuine poetry ever graces these effusions.

A second grouping which Professor Panchenko isolates occupies an intermediate position from the point of view of verse technique between the "Bureaucrat school" and the practitioners of genuine syllabic verse. This group centers on the Monastery of the Resurrection founded by Patriarch Nikon, and usually known as the "New Jerusalem."[12] To this monastery the Patriarch retired when in 1658 he renounced his office, and here he remained until his condemnation in 1666; in 1681 he was permitted by Tsar Fyodor to return, but died on the way.

The New Jerusalem Monastery has a prominent place in the history of Russian church music. Here Ukrainian and Polish modes of singing, including the use of polyphony, were introduced, and poets of the monastery turned their hands to the composition of hymns in the western style. One of the most successful of these hymn writers was the monk German (d. 1682), a favorite of Nikon. To German are attributed fourteen hymns and three epitaphs —two for his friend Nikon and one for himself.

German's hymns were composed in honor of the Virgin, of various saints, the twelve festivals of the Church, etc. Like the work of other minor poets of this circle, such as the Archimandrite Tikhon, the deacon Ioanniky, the monk Vasily, etc., German's hymns were written in isosyllabic verse, or at least approach this as an ideal. In many instances the texts have been badly garbled in transmission, or in the case of the epitaphs, by the stonecutter who inscribed them on the gravestones. Such corruptions are plainly revealed by the presence of incorrect letters in the acrostics which always form a part of the verses. It is thus not always certain whether German adhered in all cases strictly to the rule of isosyllabism, or deviated from it occasionally. In any event, the verses themselves, both hymns and epitaphs, even when the lines are not absolutely equal in number of syllables, never give the effect of mere rhymed prose, as do those of the "bureaucratic school." The hymns are usually strophic in form, with lines alternating between longer and shorter, and rhymed. The acrostics are also, with the New Jerusalem group of poets, habitually rhymed, which is almost never the case with the "bureaucratic school." Among the acrostics found in German's verses there is considerable range, as e.g. from the simple: *German monakh moliasia pisakh*, "I, German the monk, wrote, praying," to the lengthy:

Plavaia vodoiu	[Swimming in water,
omyvaema toboiu	being washed by Thee,
zria tu umersha	beholding that dead one,
pisasha virsha	German wrote verses
German ridaia	sobbing,
poia i vzdykhaia	singing and sighing.]

A typical example of German's ecclesiastical verse is the following paraphrase of Psalm 140; the acrostic, reading the first letter of each line in sequence from top to bottom, is the simple verse quoted above: "I, German the monk, wrote, praying":[13]

Lord, I have cried out to Thee, give ear unto me,
 When I call out unto Thee, Thyself hearken to me,
Take my hand in loving kindness,
 Accept [my] service of prayer.
For if Thou dost not give ear to me,
 I have no other refuge.

108

With Thee I shatter the wicked foe.
Chasten me, O righteous one, Thyself in kindness,
  King of angels and of all, in goodness.
Christ, deliver me freely from the eternal torments.

Let my prayer be made straight,
  Let it be fragrant from Thee in the censer
With love, as to an acceptable sacrifice
  Show kindness even as exceptional.
Nowhere indeed shall I find a savior,
  As I know Thee [to be] the only God.
For if I have consorted with the sinful,
  I have never been sundered from the faith,
For if Thou lookest with wrath upon our sin,
  Straightway there is but little gain in all.
Christ, renew me with resurrection.

C. Writers of Syllabic Verse

The central figure of Russian verse-writing during the last third of the seventeenth century is the Belorussian monk Simeon Polotsky (1629-1680).[14] In various relationships with him and with each other are the several other important figures of the period, Sylvester Medvedev, Karion Istomin, Andrei Belobotsky, Dimitry Tuptalo of Rostov, and Stefan Yavorsky. While they cannot be regarded in quite the sense of a "school," this group of poets has, as Panchenko points out, several common features: all of them are monks, except Belobotsky; most of them are in one way or another connected with the Muscovite court; they are closely associated with educational enterprises, etc. Their court associations are so important that before any attempt is made to consider their work in detail, it will be necessary to review briefly the political history of the time of their activity.

Tsar Alexei Mikhailovich (1645-76), the second Romanov autocrat, left at his death three sons and several daughters. He had been twice married, to ladies of important boyar families: first to Maria Miloslavskaya (1648-1669), and after her death to Natalya Naryshkina (1671-1694). His eldest son Alexei Alexeevich died before his father; the second, Fyodor (III), who succeeded him in 1676, was a weak, sickly young man who succumbed at the age of 20 (1682). The third son, Ivan, was also sickly and feeble-minded besides. By his second marriage Alexei had a vigorous and intelligent son, Peter, who was, however, at the time of his half-brother's death only ten years old (born in 1672). Under these circumstances, the succession being in dispute between two claimants, one feeble-minded but mature, the other normal but an infant, the genuine power inevitably was an apple of contention between the two noble families of Miloslavsky and Naryshkin. In each case a woman was the focus of the party pretensions. The one strong, intelligent and competent child of the thirteen which Tsar Alexei had fathered by his first wife was the eldest daughter, Sophia. On the Naryshkin side the Tsaritsa Natalya was alive, and backed by several powerful relatives. The Naryshkins had the initial advantage, and obtained recognition of young Peter as Tsar in 1682; but their rivals, assisted by some of the capital garrison, the *streltsy* or "musketeers,"contrived a coup d'état in which several of the Naryshkins were killed, and obtained confirmation of their candidate as Tsar, under the title of Ivan V. By a compromise presently effected, both Ivan V and Peter I retained the dignity of Tsar, and Sophia became regent. The Naryshkins, including Peter and his mother, were removed from the capital and from any participation in affairs. Sophia had the assistance not only of her Miloslavsky relatives, but of her lover, Prince V.V. Golitsyn, an enlightened and western-oriented statesman who succeeded in negotiating an "eternal peace" with Poland in 1686, but failed miserably in two attacks on the Turkish-supported Tatars of the Crimea.

By 1689 young Peter was 17 and the Naryshkin clan, emboldened by the débâcle of Sophia's Crimean ventures, were agitating for an end of the regency. Sophia decided to forestall any such event and laid plans to seize Peter and his mother. Warned by sympathizers, they fled to the Trinity Monastery of St. Sergius, and the Naryshkin adherents, supported by some "Germans" from the foreign quarter *(nemetskaia sloboda,* "the German suburb," where young Peter had spent a great deal of his time) of Moscow overthrew Sophia and her family. Sophia was sent to spend the rest of her life in the Novodevichy Convent, and the Tsarina Natalya, as representative of her family, assumed the direction of the state. The harmless Ivan V was allowed to remain as one of the titular Tsars. Peter, absorbed in such projects as building and sailing boats, let his mother rule until her death in 1694. When his half-brother died two years later (1696), Peter became sole autocrat of Muscovy and ruled until his death in 1725. It should be emphasized that in all this rather confused period the young man who was to be the "transformer" of Russia played a very passive part. The victory of 1689 was that of the Naryshkin family; and strangely enough, in view of Peter's later position toward the church, the Patriarch Ioachim, an arch-conservative and sworn enemy of all western innovations, was Peter's supporter. No one in 1689 had any intimation of the direction which the new reign would take; and when Ioachim died in 1690, his successor Adrian, the last Patriarch (1690-1700) continued the support of the Church.

Simeon Polotsky (1629-1680: his secular name was Samuil Emelyanovich Sitnyanovich-Petrovsky; he was a native of the Belorussian town of Polotsk) was educated, like several others of the group, in the Mogila Academy of Kiev. He attracted the attention of Tsar Alexei in 1656, and was brought by him to Moscow (1664), where he remained the rest of his life. In 1665 he founded the Zaikonospassky School in the monastery of that name, which became a principal center in Moscow for "westernizing" and progressive studies. At the Tsar's orders Simeon became tutor for the crown prince Alexei, and after his premature death, for his successor the future Tsar Fyodor Alexeevich. Sylvester Medvedev (1641-1691: secular name Semyon Agafonikovich Medvedev) was a native of Kursk, a Great Russian town on the edge of the Ukraine. He served in Moscow first as a secular clerk in one of the important government bureaus *(Prikaz tainykh del),* and during this service (1665-68) attended the Zaikonospassky School, where he became Simeon Polotsky's favorite pupil. Probably under Simeon's urging his young friend retired to Putivl in 1672 and

111

became a monk under the name of Sylvester. During a visit to Moscow in 1677 Medvedev became acquainted with the new Tsar, Fyodor, who ordered him to remain in the capital as Simeon's colleague in the direction of the Zaikonospassky School. This position he continued to hold during the regency of Sophia.

During the regency there was talk of founding a Moscow University on western lines. Simeon Polotsky had died in 1680, and Sylvester Medvedev was obviously the man best qualified to head this. He composed an elaborate project for such a University, and in pleas to Sophia in prose and verse, advocated its execution. His pleas were in vain, although the regent was probably favorably disposed. The chief opposition came from the intensely Grecophile Patriarch Ioachim. It was at this time that a theological quarrel broke into the open between the "Latinizers," such as Simeon and Medvedev, and the adherents of the Byzantine tradition, such as the Patriarch, over the timing of the miracle of transsubstantiation. This purely theological squabble was complicated by a political one: the Patriarch had the support of the Naryshkin faction, as has been noted, and this faction had by this time become so powerful that Sophia and her Miloslavsky and Golitsyn adherents were almost helpless. When in August 1689 the regency was overthrown, Medvedev's fate was sealed. He fled, was arrested, and after detention in a monastery under sentence of death for over a year, was beheaded on Red Square in February 1691.

Karion Istomin Zaulonsky (c. 1650-1717), like Medvedev a native of Kursk, had a remote connection by marriage with the older scholar. He appeared in Moscow around the year 1679, having already taken monastic vows. In Moscow he was assigned a place in 1682 in the Government Printing Office (*Pechatnyi Dvor*), which had been the center, it will be recalled, for the first school of pre-syllabic poets. Already a person of considerable education, Istomin attended Medvedev's Academy in 1686, and busied himself translating various theological works from the Latin. He was an adroit diplomat, and avoided linking himself too definitively to one party; thus he was able to survive the overthrow of Sophia and the Golitsyns, his patrons, and even, under the patriarchate of Adrian (1690-1700) to acquire renewed influence with the court. He petitioned unsuccessfully to the new regent, the Tsarina Natalya, Peter's mother, for an appointment as tutor of Peter's young son, the Tsarevich Alexei, but apparently did give the prince some private lessons in versification. The death of his patron Adrian in 1700 terminated Istomin's public career, although he continued for another seventeen years to compose both verse and prose.

Mention has been made earlier of the project dear to the heart of Sylvester Medvedev, for the opening of a Moscow University. At a time when there was still some possibility of this, in 1681, Medvedev was disconcerted by the appearance in Moscow of a learned Pole named Jan Bielobocki.[15] This man had acquired a splendid western education during fifteen years of study in France, Brandenburg, Italy and Spain. He had for some time attended the Spanish University of Valladolid. He knew, besides Polish, Russian and Church Slavonic, also the languages of western Europe where he had studied—Latin, French and Italian. A short account of his earlier life, written in 1682, has recently been discovered and published. It is of some interest for his literary career:

At the inquest [October 14, 1682, in the *Posolskii Prikaz*] he stated: That by birth he was a nobleman of the Przemysl province, his father Khrishtop Belobotsky was in the service of the [Polish] King's Majesty as a cavalry officer, and that his father had been dead for 26 years. And his father's estates were in the Przemysl province, the village of Patsla. And after his father's death his mother Andreevna and his younger brother Pavel were left. And shortly after his father's death his mother also died. And his brother Pavel served in Warsaw as a jurist. And he, Andrei, left Poland seventeen years ago to learn the science of philosophy and theology, and he was in the lands of France, Italy and Spain, and studied those sciences. And it is now three years since he had come from Spain to Riga, and from Riga to Smolensk. And from Smolensk he had come to Moscow with the archbishop of Smolensk, Simeon, a year ago [1681], in February, and the archbishop of Smolensk had introduced him to the Great Sovereign, Tsar and Great Prince of blessed memory, Fyodor Alexeevich, autocrat of all Great, Little and White Russia. And at the express command of the said Great Sovereign he was living at the house of the conciliar secretary [*dumnyi diak*] Lukyan Golosov for the past half year. And in the previous year [1681] when the Great Sovereign of blessed memory had been pleased to be on his royal excursion to Vladimir, at his, the Great Sovereign's, command the same Simeon, metropolitan of Smolensk, anointed him, Andrei, with the holy oil from the Roman faith to the holy Orthodox Christian faith of the Greek rite; and in the Roman faith his, Andrei's, name was Ivan [i.e., Jan]. And after this at the

113

express command of the Great Sovereign of blessed memory he, Andrei, was assigned to the boyar Prince Mikhail Yurevich Dolgoruky, and was enrolled in the *Razriad* [the Central Administrative Bureau] in charge of the gentry list. . . . And he, Andrei, is now living in Moscow at the palace of the metropolitan of Smolensk.[16]

This highly educated and ambitious foreigner was obviously a dangerous competitor for Sylvester if a university were opened. The latter took a decisive step to combat his rival: he suborned a professional informer to denounce the Pole as a heretic, even demanding the death penalty. Somehow Belobotsky evaded the danger, but of course the "University" was never opened; instead two conservative Greeks, the brothers Likhudy, opened under the patronage of Patriarch Ioachim, a "Latin-Greek-Slavonic Academy," which was actually no more than a theological seminary. Belobotsky, under the protection apparently of his patron Dolgoruky, had the courage to engage in a public debate with the Likhudy brothers on the question of transsubstantiation, defending the Latin position. The results of this debate are known only from the writings of the Likhudy brothers, who naturally represent it as their triumph. Belobotsky, unlike the other syllabic poets, never became a monk; he married a priest's daughter and shortly afterward was sent by Sophia on the mission to China which was to negotiate the Treaty of Nerchinsk (1689). Belobotsky's position was as Latin interpreter, the Chinese representatives at the conference being mostly Jesuit missionaries. He was thus out of the country during the crucial time when the regent was overthrown. The mission returned to Moscow in 1691, after which time there is no documentary evidence on Belobotsky, though it is quite certain that he lived and worked into the 1700s.

Belobotsky's prose works, which are quite extensive, are mostly translations from the Latin: three books of Thomas à Kempis's *Imitatio Christi* (1684-85); the *Ars brevis* and the *Rhetorica* of Ramón Lull, and probably the *Ars magna* of the same great Catalan philosopher (1698-99).

The monk—and saint of the Orthodox church—Dimitry Rostovsky[17] (1651-1709) was born Daniil Savvich Tuptalo, son of a Cossack aristocrat of the Kiev region. He studied for three years at the Mogila Academy in Kiev, after which he took monastic vows. He soon acquired fame as an ecclesiastical orator, and served in

1677-79 as a preacher in Slutsk. In 1682 Dimitry conceived the idea of compiling a prose version of saints' lives arranged according to the calendar of their festival days—the so-called *Chet'ii Minei*. He began the work in 1684, and brought it to completion in 1705. As a result of the intense labor expended on the *Minei* Dimitry was reluctant to undertake the duties to which an appointment by Tsar Peter in 1700 assigned him—as metropolitan of Tobolsk in Siberia. With the help of his friend Stefan Yavorsky, then *locum tenens* of the vacant patriarchate, Dimitry obtained instead the metropolitan's chair of Rostov, a post to which he owes the name usually given him. In Rostov he founded a school in which were taught Latin, Greek and Church Slavonic, and for which Dimitry composed verses and dramas. This side of his production will be considered later.

The last important poet of the seventeenth century belongs more to the realm of Neo-Latin than Russian literature—Stefan (Simeon) of Yavor in Galicia (Stefan Yavorsky, 1658-1722).[18] Like the other Ukrainian poets of the century, he was educated in the Mogila Academy. He then, for further training, attended various Jesuit schools in Poland-Lithuania, which necessitated his conversion to Catholicism. Returning with a Master of Arts degree to Kiev, he was reconverted to Orthodoxy and became a monk. His verses in Polish, Latin and Church Slavonic won him the honorary title of *Poeta laureatus*. At the death in 1700 of Patriarch Adrian, Tsar Peter, who was determined to reorganize the Russian church and put it in a distinctly subordinate position, appointed Yavorsky as director (president) of the Holy Synod and *locum tenens* of the vacant patriarchal see. This post he held for the rest of his life, although relations with Peter became more and more strained. Stefan held Catholic views on the superiority of the spiritual to the secular power, and abhorred Peter's western reforms. He was thus thrown into the camp of the conservatives who surrounded the Tsarevich Alexei, and when the Tsarevich was arrested for treason (1718) Stefan's authority was severely curtailed; while he continued to hold his official position, the actual administration of the Holy Synod was managed by Peter's staunch adherent Feofan Prokopovich, Yavorsky's nominal subordinate. Most of Yavorsky's poetical output is in Latin or Polish; he was particularly renowned for his fine and moving Latin elegy "To his Library" *(Possessoris horum librorum luctuosum libris vale*—"Mournful Farewell to [his] Books by the Possessor of These Books").

Some of the general characteristics of the syllabic poets of the last third of the seventeenth century can be gathered from the above sketch of their activities. With the exception of the Pole Belobotsky all were monks; not until after the reforms of Peter do we find the medieval church monopoly of literature broken. In keeping with the ecclesiastical character of the poets, their themes are exclusively religious and didactic. They are all associated with educational enterprises, either as teachers in public institutions or as private tutors of royalty. All without exception are "westernizers" by education, if not by actual origin (except for Medvedev and Istomin, all are either Belorussian, Ukrainian or Polish by birth). They are oriented toward the Latin culture of the West rather than toward the traditional Byzantine culture of old Muscovy. In this respect the conflict between Medvedev and Istomin on the one side, and the Likhudy brothers on the other is symbolic.

No plainer clue to the nature of syllabic poetry in general can be found than the early backgrounds of these poets. This kind of verse is exotic and has no genuine Russian roots. There is, of course, a certain kinship between it and the pre-syllabic verse of the first part of the century, but no genetic connection. It is significant that pre-syllabic verse continues to be composed, for certain purposes, even during the heyday of syllabic verse. There is very little interpenetration; they are distinct species.

The basis of syllabic verse is isosyllabism; we have seen this in the "spiritual songs" of the New Jerusalem school, where it is almost certainly a western import. The background of all the important syllabic poets in the practice of Latin and Polish verse is the direct impulse toward the new form. Syllabic poetry, as it is seen in the exceedingly voluminous work of Simeon Polotsky, its Russian initiator, is marked by syllable-counting and by terminal rhyme, and by disregard of the Russian word-accent. Rhyme is normally, though not exclusively, feminine, as it always is in Polish. In longer lines, those of thirteen syllables for example, there is always an obligatory caesura (after the seventh syllable), which helps to stabilize the otherwise extremely flaccid verse. Some exotic verse forms, such as the Sapphic strophe (obviously imported from Latin hymnography) appear, but even here the rule of couplet rhyme is observed (see e.g. Simeon Polotsky's poem "The Carefree Debtor" [Panchenko, no. 42]).

The genres which the syllabic poets cultivated run a considerable gamut. There are congratulatory verses (ancestors of the eighteenth-century "ode"), epistles, lamentations, epitaphs, emblematic verses (that is, epigrams composed as explanations of coats-of-arms—usually imaginary—of highly placed persons), epigrams, paraphrases of Psalms, etc. Unique in their kind are Simeon Polotsky's enormous collection of edifying anecdotes, the "Garden of Many Flowers," the versified *Domostroi* of Karion Istomin, and Belobotsky's *Pentateugum*, or "Five Books on the Four Last Things and the Vanity and Life of Man." Some of the syllabic poets, e.g. Simeon Polotsky, not content with ornamenting their verse with acrostics, composed poems in various symbolic shapes—a tree, a cross, a heart—or the like.

1. Simeon Polotsky

The monk Simeon of Polotsk[19] must have been one of the most prolific Russian writers of all time. His close friend and admirer Sylvester Medvedev, who shared a cell with him in the Zaikonospassky Monastery, records that Simeon had a vow to write daily, in a very fine hand, what amounts to eight modern notebook pages. A.M. Panchenko refuses to characterize this as "graphomania," but it certainly comes perilously close. Outside of the 50,000 or more verses with which his latest editor credits him, he composed dramas, to which we shall return later, and a voluminous output of religious prose, e.g. a tract against the Old Ritualists ("The Rod of Governance," 1667), two collections of sermons ("Spiritual Dinner" and "Spiritual Supper," 1682-83), etc. All his work, whether prose or verse, is equally didactic in purpose. The force that drove Simeon to his intense productivity was a laudable desire to bring enlightenment to his backward countrymen. In this desire there was nothing of the egoist: Simeon had no thought of leaving behind him a *mnema eis aei*, or *monumentum aere perennius*. He was animated only by fear that like the unfaithful steward in Jesus's parable, he might be charged at the Terrible Judgment with not having used his "talent" to the

117

fullest.

A collection of Simeon's verse was issued just before his death, in 1678-79, under the title *Ritmologion.* It contains some 1500 pieces, in various genres, many of them written for public occasions in a form which is directly ancestral to the eighteenth-century ode, e.g. of Trediakovsky or Lomonosov. A typical example is the long poem dedicated, in an equally long explanatory title, to Tsar Alexei Mikhailovich on the occasion of the completion of his famous baroque palace at Kolomenskoe.[20] In another Simeon celebrates the "Russian Eagle,"[21] and finds all the worthies of antiquity—Arion, Amphion, Demosthenes, Cicero, Homer, Virgil and Ovid—incapable of doing justice to the greatness of Tsar Alexei. Besides the "occasional poems" of this kind, the *Ritmologion* contains Simeon's two extant dramas, "Comedy on Nebuchadnezzar," and "Comedy of the Prodigal Son."

The second collection of Polotsky's work in verse is the *Vertograd mnogotsvetnyi,* or the "Garden of Many Flowers."[22] There are 1246 of these "flowers," ranging widely in length, from couplets to poems running to several hundred lines. The arrangement is based on the alphabet, with entries e.g. from "Alexander" and "Augustus" to "Phaedra," "Man" *(chelovek),* "Youth" *(iunost'),* etc. The sources of these anecdotes and similar material are of all kinds and periods—ancient writers like Pliny the Elder and Aelian, medieval encyclopedists like Vincent of Beauvais, historians, saints' lives, church fathers, etc. The intent is obviously to be encyclopedic, to compress into the compass of a single—albeit gigantic—book all the knowledge that an educated man should need. A couple of examples will suffice to show both the metrical and the "poetical" characteristics of Polotsky's verse.

The entry devoted in this encyclopedia to the "Earth" *(zemlia)* is surprisingly short for the magnitude of the subject—one Sapphic stanza. Sappho's lovely stanza has had some very strange mutations in the course of the centuries, from Catullus's *Ille mi par esse deo videtur* to the "Sapphische Ode" that Johannes Brahms immortalized in a great song. Polotsky's is perhaps the oddest of all. It derives from such a Latin hymn as "Ut queant laxis resonare fibris," either directly or through a Polish intermediary. The eleven-syllable line of the Latin is preserved, and the "adonic verse" that ends the classical strophe is approximated with a five-syllable last line; the four lines rhyme in couplets:[23]

zemlia tri chasti moknut pod vodami,
chetverta tokmo sukha pod nogami
vsekh est' khodiashchikh i razum imushchikh,
i zverei sushchikh.

[Three parts (i.e., quarters) of the earth are wet, beneath waters. only the fourth is dry, beneath the feet of all that walk and possess reason, and (such as) are animals.]

Polotsky's most commonly employed verse is the 13-syllable couplet-rhyming line, with a caesura after the seventh syllable. From a cycle of verses on the important subject "Wealth" *(bo-gatstvo)* comes this brief poem, of which the first two lines will suffice to show the meter of the original, as well as the pun:

> Ellinom bogatstv bóg be, / narechenyi Plúton.
> Az ego imenúiu / voistinu plút on.

It will be seen that the strong caesura cuts each line into two hemistichs; the word accent plays no part except for the end of the line and the position just before the caesura, where it must fall on the penult. The effect of such a line is likely to remind an English-speaking person of such a nursery-rhyme as "The queen was in the parlor, eating bread and honey." In the two lines here quoted the poet resorts to the famous classical procedure of finding an omen in a name *(nomen omen)*:

The Hellenes [i.e., pagan Greeks] had a god of riches named Pluton.
I name him: in truth a rascal [is] he *[plut on]*,
For he cheats needlessly and entangles greatly
In devilish toils which take captive.
They used to paint him as lame, when he would enter a house,
And winged, when he would go out from there,
Meaning to signify that gaining riches is slow,
But their disappearance is speedy;
Even as they are very slowly amassed,
But often disappear in a single hour.
And even if they do serve one to the end [of his life],
Yet after death one must needs be deprived of them.[24]

Another very short verse on a very important subject is the Sapphic

119

stanza on "Death":

> A soldier does not have the least pleasure
> When an enemy with a sword catches him.
> Everyman [vsiak cheloveche], behold: after you is coming
> Death with a scythe.[25]

The rare occasions when any of Simeon's competently constructed *virshi* resembled real poetry are mostly those where the majestic phraseology of the Psalter shines through them. Such, for example, is the "Prayer of Saint Ioasaph as he enters the wilderness."[26] St. Ioasaph, it may be remembered, is a Christianized version of Gautama Buddha, whose very popular legend, "Varlaam and Ioasaph," records the conversion of the Indian prince by the Christian Varlaam, and his retirement to a hermit's life in the forest. The Muscovite prose version of the "Tale of Varlaam and Ioasaph," published in 1680, contained a lengthy verse "prayer," composed by Simeon Polotsky. This is written in a short eight-syllable line without caesura, rhyming as usual in couplets. The movement of the verse is strongly trochaic, and it gives the effect of an accentual trochaic tetrameter, with leonine rhyme, taking the paired lines together, as in the Latin hymn: *Pange, lingua, gloriosi proelium certaminis*:

> Bozhe otche vsemogushchii, Bozhe syne prisnosushchii,
> Bozhe dushe paraklite, mnogozarnyi mira svete,
> V triekh litsekh prebyvaiai, sushchestvo si tozhde znaiai!

God the Father Almighty, God the Son from Everlasting,
God the Spirit, the Comforter, brightly shining light for the world,
Existing in three persons, knowing existence for Thyself likewise!.
To Thee I, a sinner, come [and] I shed many tears:
Deign to receive me that I may serve Thee.
As soon as Thou shalt give life, I desire to be Thy servant forever.

2. Sylvester Medvedev

Simeon's favorite disciple and friend, Sylvester Medvedev,[27] endeavored to emulate his master as closely as possible; he was, however, altogether left behind in the matter of literary quantity. Qualitatively, on the other hand, he is often Simeon's superior.

As a pious memorial to the older poet Sylvester composed his *Epitafion*, a cycle of short verse "epitaphs," seemingly modeled on the tradition of the Greek sepulchral epigram. The first and the eleventh of these may represent their general character:

> Beholding this tomb, O man, let your heart be moved;
> Shed tears for the death of the glorious teacher.
> For here is a teacher who was the only one such,
> A righteous theologian, who kept the Church's dogmas.
>
> He committed his soul into the hand of God Almighty,
> Who had deigned to give it, being immortal.
> May He receive it as His own creation
> And fulfill its desire for eternal blessings.[28]

A relatively brief but characteristic sample of the congratulatory address to royalty, which was a very popular genre with the court poets of the age and directly ancestral to the laudatory ode of the next century, is Sylvester's "Greeting to the Tsarevna Sophia on the Occasion of Easter" (1685).[29]

> The day of bright light shines in the world,
> With the light of the spirit it illumines our race,
> With the grace of eternal God,
> And it shows the path to the mansion above,
> Which had been destroyed while still in Eden
> When the serpent tempted Eve and Adam,
> So that Christ God might create this day,
> Might appoint it for us as a path to Him in heaven.
> Moreover He is also a good guide unto all
> Who but hearken attentively to Him.
> But you, O great and glorious Tsarevna,
> Wise Sophia Alexeevna,
> Hearken earnestly to Him who is risen
> And zealously perform His will,
> And you walk on the path appointed by Him,
> And thus you will enter into the light all-desired,
> The same shall not grow pale for all ages,
> And there you shall shine like the sun.
> This I zealously desire for you,

121

Our sovereign lady, here and in heaven.
And be pleased to spare me in kindness,
Who desire to be your faithful slave forever.
And now I make my profound obeisance,
I lower my head to your feet.

The human side of the divine drama of the crucifixion is seldom emphasized in older Orthodox art and literature. Thus, in the eleventh-century mosaics in the monastery church at Daphni, near Athens, the Virgin and St. John stand beside the crucified Christ, their faces expressive not of grief and compassion, but of recognition of the magnitude of the love of the God on the cross. Already by the fourteenth century, as in the frescoes at Nerezi in Yugoslavia, the sorrow of Jesus's mother at her Son's agony finds pictorial and moving representation. By the seventeenth century, partly under western influence no doubt, the figure of the *Mater dolorosa* becomes a familiar one in religious verse in Orthodox, as in Catholic lands. One of the most poignant of such representations is Sylvester Medvedev's "Verses for Holy Saturday" *(virsha v velikuiu subbotu)*, from which come the following lines:

All the hearts of the faithful shed tears, but most of all the Mother
Will not cease for even a little from bitter tears.
Streams of bitter tears in wailing she pours forth,
And mourns thus from a heart that is moved:
"O sweet my Son, Son all-beloved,
Begotten without husband, without birth-pangs born!
How have you deigned to endure these sufferings,—
Creature has slain its Creator, children their Father.
O sweet child, divine child,
In joy begotten, born in mirth!
In vain does grief now fill my heart,
The sword that Simeon prophesied pierces it.
Seeing you dead, how can I be alive?
Without my Life I do not wish to live.
Light of my eyes, how have you set?
Wherefore have you taken me into the grave and Hell with you?
Without you the sun is darkness to me, the darkness with you is light,
With you I lived on earth as though in heaven.
Soothe my tears, child, for I shall sob,
Until you rise from the tomb!"[30]

122

3. Karion Istomin

Karion Istomin's[31] quite extensive literary production is thus summarized in the headnote to the Panchenko-Adrianova-Peretts edition of *Syllabic Poets of the XVIIth and XVIIIth Centuries*:[32]

> Following the example of Sylvester Medvedev, Karion came forward in the role of court poet and orator. He composed sermons for various occasions, wrote panegyrics (beginning with a book of salutatory verses presented to the Tsarevna Sophia in 1681) and epitaphs, he worked in the epigrammatic genre (verses on "coats-of-arms" and inscriptions for ikons), he loved the spiritual lyric and even tried his powers in the genre of the heroic poem, attempting "in measured lines" to depict the second Crimean expedition of Prince V.V. Golitsyn. Besides this, Istomin worked zealously as a translator from the Latin. In 1687, for example, he presented to the Tsarevna Sophia a work of St. Augustine (or pseudo-Augustine), called in translation "God-seen Love"; he was active as a historiographer.

After Peter's accession to real power, Karion composed a number of primers and other pedagogical works in an effort to win place as tutor for the child Alexei Petrovich. It was perhaps in connection with this design that he composed the so-called "verse Domostroi" (1696).

The original "Domostroi" (the Slavonic word is an attempt to render the Greek *oikonomos*, i.e., "household manager") was a sixteenth-century work attributed to the priest Sylvester, who was for a few early years a trusted adjutant of Ivan the Terrible.[33] The work, in prose, sets forth the proper behavior, according to the Muscovite traditions, of all the members of a household, and especially in their relations with the master of the house. Needless to say the Russian *pater familias* had power of all but life and death in the family, his wife and children being in little better position in this regard than his serfs. Karion's versified "Domostroi," somewhat more methodical though no less severe than the original, provides systematically at the end of each of the 12-line stanzas in which he prescribes a child's conduct, alternative punishments for infraction of the rules laid down in that stanza:

123

so many "blows" or "wounds" administered with the rod, or so many "prostrations" (*poklony*) to an ikon. Beginning his work with a disarming jingle, Istomin writes:

> Siiu dshchitsu vziav v desnitsu,
> Chti i pomni stikhi slovni,
> Mal i staryi v razum pravyi.

> [Picking up this tablet in your right hand,
> Read and remember these oral verses,
> Young and old in right reason.]

The admonitions begin with the child's rising from bed [sec. 2]:

> Having arisen from sleep, as one [new] created,
> Be mindful of God, as having been appointed unto this.
> Make the sign of the holy cross with your hand upon you,
> Pray, and behold the Creator before you.
> As far as possible, keep your mind and thought,
> Do not count vanities at this time, to be your temptation.
> With prayer wash yourself, clothe yourself,
> And having combed your hair, wash your mouth; do not laugh;
> And make due obeisance to your parents,
> Show yourself with friendliness to all in the house.
> If maid or youth does not behave thus,
> He shall receive seven strokes for it.
>
> 30 prostrations.[34]

One should note the stern prohibition: "Do not laugh!" Seventeenth-century Russian decorum regarded laughter as a veritable device of the Devil for man's ensnarement. A well-known proverb runs: *"smekhi da khikhi Vvedut do grekhi"* ["Laughter and tittering lead into sin"]. The Greek Orthodox archdeacon Paul of Aleppo, who has left a lively account of his journey to Muscovy in the seventeenth century, writes of the constant espionage to which clerics are subjected for fear of their behaving in a worldly fashion. In his remarks on this head he notes: "As concerns jokes and laughter, we became completely foreign to them, because of the sly Muscovites who were keeping watch over us and observing, and reporting to the Tsar or the Patriarch everything they noted in us, good or bad. So we kept a strict check on ourselves, not of our own accord, but of necessity, and against our will conducted ourselves on the model of the lives of saints."[35] No wonder syllabic verse is almost without exception solemn and ultra-serious!

Having begun the day properly, the young person is naturally admonished to continue in the same fashion [sec. 9]:

> Pass the day in profitable activity,
> Do not roam about vainly in thought or body,—
> Maintain a pious life with holy manners,
> In pure thoughts with frequent prayers
> Maintain Christian piety,
> Learn the liberal arts *[nauk svobodnykh]* as a citizen *[grazhdansko]*,
> The breed of Christian children must not refrain from going
> into the holy church.
> It is a duty to glorify God communally *[soborne]* for everything,
> Do not unnecessarily leave off intelligent discourse.
> He who shall not attend to this with all zeal,
> Shall not escape twenty wounds.
>
> 100 prostrations.

Perhaps Karion did occasionally unbend, in company with his friends—in a perfectly orderly and godly fashion, of course! There is some slight warrant for supposing this from his epistles to others of his circle, as for instance this, composed apparently in 1706, to Dimitry Tuptalo, the metropolitan of Rostov:[36]

> Most honored Father Dimitry!
> Does it behoove us today to be in your house,
> The book upon the table to open to the words?
> If something else is ordained,
> For godly people this too is proper.
> We have not seen each other truly for a long while.
> Live many years healthy in the Lord!
> Let us keep repeating
> And bowing in love,
> The Archangel Michael
> Has revealed God to all,
> The Archangel Gabriel
> Has shown Christ in the flesh.

Paul of Aleppo's account of Muscovy, mentioned above, goes into some detail on the surveillance maintained over monastery visitors, and the suspicion of loose conduct among monks:[37]

Our guide told us [as we approached the frontier of Muscovy] that if anyone wanted to shorten his life by fifteen years, he should go into the land of the Muscovites and live among them as an ascetic, exhibiting continual continence and fasting, busying himself with prayer, and rising at midnight. He must eschew joking, laughter, and familiarity—because the Muscovites post supervisors with the archpriests and monasteries and they watch over all who travel thither, by night and day, through keyholes, observing whether they are behaving themselves decorously in humility, silence, fasting and prayer, or are indulging in drunkenness, amusing themselves with gambling, jesting, laughing or cursing. . . .

Naturally such calumnies aroused resentment and protest among the monastic men of letters, and Karion Istomin composed this indignant rebuttal:[38]

Many tell	what monks do
Where in the monastery	they have no task.
That they sit, forsooth,	and know nothing
Of how to honor	God, and pay obeisance.
It behooves one	to experience for himself
And in a monastery	to spend even a little time.
He will learn how	one lives in the cell.
How he renounces	designs and passions.
For it is impossible	for one not to learn,
Not to show himself	a warrior in spiritual battle.
Thoughts are troubled	in the souls of the learned
	[slovesnykh]
And in worldly people;	they will not stay in the righteous.
One must speak	with care
Not find fault	in any sort of foolishness.

Behold this and learn, slander no one.
God will give justification to all
Unto their saintly glory.

The monastery gates	are locked
For the life of monks	is perfected in God.
Whosoever shall have	love for God
Let him as a monk	sit in a cell
For he will learn	how life wears on,
And patience	that he may be saved forever.

("On What is Reported by People, How Monks Live in the Monastery")

126

4. Dimitry Rostovsky

Most of the literary activity of Dimitry Rostovsky[39] was expended on his enormous prose compilation, the calendar of saint's lives *(Chet'ii Minei)*. He also, as has been noted, composed some works in dramatic form to be performed by the pupils of his Rostov school. To these we shall return later. His non-dramatic verse output is not large: there are occasional verses in his prose letters, and he wrote paraphrases of the Psalms which were sung by the monks of his Rostov monastery. One *kant*, or "spiritual song," to his patron saint, Dimitry of Thessalonica, is given in the Panchenko anthology; its first few lines are as follows:[40]

> The good warrior, chosen for the King
> Jesus Christ, not trampled on by the foe,
> The glory of the martyr Dmitry let us honor,
> And let us twine for him a crown of songs.
> Triumph eternally over the host of foes,
> Rejoice amid the choirs of angels,
> Thou who didst love Jesus as a sweetheart
> And who didst lay down thy life for His honor!
> Imitate Him who was pierced by the spear,
> Who, thirsting, was given to drink gall with a sponge;
> For the sweet one he [i.e. Dmitry] gave himself over to bitter wounds,
> Confessing Christ before the tyrant.

5. Stefan Yavorsky

Stefan Yavorsky,[41] though a very important literary and political figure of the end of the seventeenth century, has greater renown as a writer of Latin verse than Russian. His most famous poem is the Latin elegy in which he bids farewell to his beloved library as death approaches. This elegy was translated into Russian syllabic verse by a contemporary, from which Panchenko quotes fourteen lines:[42]

127

Books, so often held by me, come,
Light of my eyes, depart from me!
Depart with good fortune, satisfy others,
Pour out the drops of your juice now to others!
Woe is me! My eye is removed from you,
Nor can it be any more sated by you.
More than honey and the honeycomb were you sweet to me,
To live with you was sweet, for you took away sorrow.
You were riches, you were great glory to me,
You were Paradise, the joy of love and such great sweetness.
You made me glorious, you illuminated me,
You acquired for me graciousness with highborn persons.
But to live longer with you (Oh, heavy sorrow!)
Is forbidden by the hour of death and a sea of bitter tears.

Of his Russian poems Yavorsky's most famous is the lengthy expostulation put in the mouth of Mother Russia to the "traitor" Mazeppa, the Cossack hetman who deserted Peter the Great for Charles XII of Sweden and fought on the Swedish side at Poltava. The poem consists of eleven eight-line stanzas—a form that is quite close to the classical eighteenth-century ode, though the subject matter would certainly be inappropriate to the ode! A translation of the first two stanzas will give an adequate idea of the poet's angry eloquence:[43]

"Save me, O God," cries Russia,
"From the venomous and cruel serpent,
Whom the rivets of Hell await—
The former chieftain Ivan Mazeppa.
Oh! The poor mother suffers heavy sorrow,
A viper gnaws my womb.
Who shall give me tears, as to Rachel?
I shall weep bitterly in my troubled state.

Behold, a second Herod, filled with deadly poison—
Cruel Mazeppa has slain my children.
Russia has been made like David,
Who from his son suffered offence.
His son Absalom was ungrateful,
And like him perfidious Mazeppa;
I loved him as a mother her son—
Whence then such betrayal?"

6. Andrei Belobotsky

Russian syllabic verse is a part of the European Baroque, and there are many traits which link East and West in this area; but there are many more traits that link syllabic verse to the Middle Ages, even though, as we know, that period knew no such thing as written verse. One of the most characteristic themes of western Baroque poetry—and it marks the music and the art of the age as well—is that of the fragility of the flesh and the horror of death. Such a theme is indeed a medieval commonplace, but there is a wide divergence between the conventional *danse macabre* of the fifteenth century, even with the grisly figure of skeletal Death with his scythe, and the fascinated and morbid horror of the Baroque treatment, with its gloating enumeration of the physical aspects of decay. In Russian Baroque literature there is little of this, though the theme of *memento mori* is omnipresent. A typical example is the brief verse of Simeon Polotsky, quoted above: "Look, O man—Death is after you with a scythe!" But one poet of the period constitutes a major exception in this regard, as he does in many others. This is Jan (Andrei) Belobotsky (Polish Bielobocki),[44] whose extraordinary *Pentateugum* is a veritable "Triumph of Death." There is no doubt that this work is an exotic plant in Russian literature, and belongs by inspiration and tone more to Polish and German traditions than to those of Muscovy. Nonetheless, the work is composed in Russian syllabic verse, and if for no other reason requires mention. More than that, however—for an impartial reader, wearied beyond bearing by the flat, uninspired wastes of Simeon Polotsky's or Karion Istomin's *virshi*, is brought up with a real start when he encounters Belobotsky, for here at least is a genuine poet, not a mere versifier. He may be awkward, he may write incorrect Russian at times and intrude scraps of Polish vocabulary and morphology, his text may be corrupt and at times unintelligible—but he is, for all this, a poet who may without too great exaggeration be spoken of in the same breath with such contemporaries as Góngora and John Donne.

Belobotsky's work is one of compilation, as its Russian discoverer A. Gorfunkel has explained. The first two "cantos," which concern "Death" and "The Last Judgment," derive from a German Jesuit poet named Rader; and the second two, on "Hell" and "Heaven," from a work by another German Jesuit, Johann Niess. Gorfunkel's description will shed some light on these obscure originals: "Written in Latin verse, these four 'odes' were extremely popular and were repeatedly reissued during the course of the whole seventeenth century, both separately and together, under the common designation 'On the Four Things that Follow the Life of Man.' " Belobotsky for some reason chose to add a fifth "canto," which is a selection of 30 stanzas out of 100 from a poem of Jakob Balde (1604-1668) "On the Vanity of the World," known in both German and Latin variants, and extremely popular. The Russian *Pentateugum* ("Five Books") was apparently made from Polish translations of these Latin and German originals, the first four "odes" by Zygmunt Brudecki.

There is only one known manuscript of the poem, and it is frequently corrupt, as can be seen by the unmetrical lines, and by unintelligible passages. The meter is most unusual. The poem is divided into octaves of eight 8-syllable lines, and the lines are alternately unrhymed and rhymed (i.e., xaxa xbxb). This use of alternately rhyming and unrhymed lines is apparently not known in Russian before Belobotsky's poem, and is evidently derived from the Polish translation of Brudecki, which has an identical scheme. The Latin originals have no rhyme. As A. Gorfunkel, who first published the poem,[45] states, the writer of the unique manuscript ran each pair of lines together into a single 16-syllable line, thus forming a series of 166 quatrains, with the normal couplet rhyme, and of course a strong medial caesura. The first "Ode" consists of 23 such quatrains, the second of 40, the third of 51, the fourth of 22, and the last of 30. It is perhaps an indication of Baroque taste that the longest development is that given to "Hell"; "Heaven" receives less than half as much attention, and part even of this is devoted to descriptions of the sufferings of the blessed martyrs. The Latin original of Johann Niess shows 60 stanzas as against Belobotsky's 22 for this section.

The Latin verses of Rader and Niess, once very popular, are now little known and accessible with difficulty, and it is necessary to accept the word of A. Gorfunkel as to their literary quality. They are, according to him, undistinguished, mere "sermons in verse," cold, abstract, and lacking in all poetic character. Particularly

130

noticeable is their remoteness from every concrete feature of life. This unattractive, abstract feature of the Jesuit poets' work is already overcome, according to Gorfunkel, by the quite free translation of Zygmunt Brudecki, into which the translator was able to put a great deal of national Polish atmosphere. Belobotsky's Russian translation does the same thing; abstract "kings and princes" become "tsars and boyars," the obsequies for the dead include the *vechnaia pamiat'*, "eternal remembrance" service, the fires of Hell are compared to iron-smelters, etc. The result is a far greater degree of poetical vividness than the originals contain.

One of the most characteristic of Baroque traits, inherited in the West from the Renaissance, is the omnipresence of classical history and mythology, grotesquely juxtaposed with Christian themes. Thus Simeon Polotsky, in his poem "The Russian Eagle" has the pagan Muse Clio describe the symbolic "eagle" as assuming the vesture of Christ. Belobotsky's Hell is peopled with the creatures of classical Hades—the three-headed dog Cerberus, the thirsting Tantalus, the ferryman Charon, the fury Megaera, etc. The new arrival in Paradise is given a capsule lesson in astronomy (Canto IV, st. 3-4), with Bootes, Castor and Pollux, the Pleiades, Orion, Arcturus, etc., as adornments of a region pictured largely in terms of the heavenly city described in the Apocalypse. The fifth canto, on "The Life of Man, or Vanity," begins with the example of once proud Troy brought low, and later (V, st. 10-13) runs through several of the "seven wonders of the world," and ends with a sketchy history of Rome from Romulus to Alaric's sack. But Belobotsky, as Gorfunkel assures us, does far less of this than his Latin originals, and avoids a great deal of mythological ornamentation.

It is not surprising that a poet of Polish birth, like Belobotsky, should fail to handle the Russian language perfectly idiomatically. Aside, however, from the occasional use of a non-Russian word (e.g. *gra* for *igra*, "game," or *daremne* [i.e., *daremny*] , "in vain"), the Polish flavor of the poem probably escapes a reader to whom seventeenth-century Russian is far from a native idiom! To this linguistic element may probably be assigned the frequent and morphologically unjustified use of the dative singular noun ending -*ovi*: thus, for example, in Canto V, Strophes 14, 15 and 17 we have the following: *Novukhodonosorovi*, "To Nebuchadnezzar";

131

razumovi, "to reason"; *idolovi*, "to the idol"; *balvanovi*, "to the block," *Annibalovi*, "to Hannibal," and *grekovi*, "to the Greek." The termination of course belongs historically not to the o-declension, but to the u-declension; but *-owi* is the commonest dative singular termination of masculine nouns in Polish.

In the absence of any explanations on the nature of the *Pentateugum* manuscript, it is difficult to know what to make of the very frequent cases where lines are hypermetrical (e.g. IV, 11, line 2, which has 20 instead of 16 syllables) or hypometrical (e.g. I, 4, line 4, which has only 14 syllables; IV, 16, line 4, which has only 10). Such lines are of course impossible to read metrically; and it not seldom happens that the loss of a single syllable from somewhere in the middle of the line results in the grotesque rhyming of a masculine with a feminine ending (e.g., I, 5, 3; I, 7, 3). In places defective rhyme makes it perfectly obvious that an inattentive scribe has garbled the passage, as e.g. III, 35; here the first two lines of the strophe read:

> zbiten' s tel'nym v prasu kladut, kotly i z smoloiu *kipeiat*,
> ognia zharu pribavliaiut, telesa s dushami *variat*.

[They put *zbiten'* (a kind of mixed drink) with *tel'noe* (a fish dish) in the press, cauldrons with pitch are boiling; they add fire, heat, they boil bodies with souls.]

The unmetrical ending *kipeiat* has to be emended to *kipiat*, to rhyme with *variat* and eliminate the extra syllable. But are all such cases owing to this kind of corruption, or was the poet himself sometimes careless? He may have been, but it seems highly unlikely that any person with an ear could have been guilty of the most monstrous of these blunders; the blame should therefore probably be shifted in large part to an ignorant copyist. (Gorfunkel notes that the manuscript, though of the seventeenth century, is definitely *not* an autograph.)

The first canto, "on Death," contains some of the finest poetry, as well as some of the most characteristic features of the *Pentateugum*, and I shall therefore translate several passages from it. It begins:[46]

1. O sun, more shining than gold, O moon, pure beyond silver,
   The heart hears death close by; I must die—for you is goodly life.
   You two luminaries by day and night, your life knows no old age.
   For us the sleep of death creeps over our eyes, affrights
                          both old and young.

2. O stars, shine on in heaven, O planets, move in orbit,
   Sister Pleiades, farewell; send rain upon our fevers.
   Castor and Pollux, your kindness is evident on the sea to sailors,
   But for us the brightness of stars will not avail, as we
                          sink with the ship of life.

3. Meadows, swards, flowers, groves, fields, hills, vineyards,
   Earth and the fruits of trees, orchards, woods, gardens,
   Springs of crystal waters, meditations of sweetly-singing birds,
   The year of our life will end; bid farewell to the dying.

4. All living creatures, God help you, and you,
                          elements of animate things,
   Faintness overpowers me, death has summoned me
                          to the other world.
   All creation beneath the heavens' circle, moving in your places,
   Now and forevermore be preserved by God. [two syllables short]

5. Cruel death, bitter death sharpens his arrow and bends his bow.
   Willy-nilly, the mighty one will speedily draw me to himself.
   Neither by entreaty nor by threat is it possible to
                          make terms with him;
   He receives no gifts, but cuts with his scythe, he plunders endlessly.

6. Soon there will be knocking at the door, say farewell to your life.
   When you die, you will cease to be called brother to your friends.
   Alas, you are departing on a far journey, and you
                          have but little store,
   You will not take money thither, [your] deeds
                          alone remain with you.

7. The face melts down like wax, the bright eyes are darkened,
   Your breath is locked in your throat, tongue, mouth grow numb.
   The color will fall away from the face, the veins
                          are robbed of blood.
   You are pale, dear brother, when Charon appears to you.

8. Hard will be the bed to the head, pleasant as salt in one's eyes,
   Friends formerly speak to your glory, now,
                          O dead man, in dark night.
   Today everyone bows to the face of the earth for your favor,
   Tomorrow you will lie under the ground, and
                          ingratitude is in their hearts.

133

9. With your stench you will repel all, they will
                                    hold their noses and mouths,
   You will not incline their friendliness, they will say to
                                    you as they turn away:
   "Away from the house, aye, away from the court!
                                    Why keep a corpse?
   See, he has rotted, it is time to bury him, it is time for
                                    him to sleep in the ground."
10. When the breath goes out of you, they will toss
                                    you into the dark tomb.
   Weeping and sobbing will go up, wife and children
                                    will abandon you.
   When they have buried your body in the ground,
                                    and sung the requiem,
   At dinner they will laugh at your nearness, forgetting you.
11. In your coffin every reptile, worms, mice with frogs
   Will live, my lord—serpents with vipers will stand guard.
   Such will be your court and courtiers, the troops,
                                    the regiments around you;
   Prepare their wages for them, for their provisions give—yourself.

The physical horror, ugliness and grotesqueness of death could scarcely be more drastically depicted than in these verses. At the same time the familiar satirical theme of the forgetfulness of the living, even of the wife and children of the dead, is woven in, to emphasize the contrast between life and death. These are Baroque commonplaces, and mark much of the moralizing verse of other poets of the age, e.g. Simeon Polotsky, but nowhere as powerfully as here.

The terrors of the Last Judgment follow, in the second canto of the poem; the description is inspired, of course, by the Apocalypse:[47]

2. The heart trembles, thought is confused, the
                                    tongue breaks off a word,
   Terror torments my belly, my breath is caught in my throat,
   Jests, amusements, joys—flee far from me,
   Veins burst, bones dry up; eyes, pour forth tears.
3. Wherever I gaze, everywhere terror, fright, sickness, tumult;
   There stands the fiery rod, punishment for the sinful.
   The planets, the stars have gone out, the sun, the moon grown dark,
   The wild winds have become more terrible, earthquakes

have created chasms.

4. The sea boils, the granite is shattered, sweats marvelously,
   There are cries, wails and great noise, and the heavenly firmament
   trembles [Polish *khveet*]
   The earth has fallen with its feet upward, it is trans-
   formed with all its cities,
   The remnant burns, and we with it, the living dead.
5. Silence reigns in the world, burned to ashes to the [last] stick,
   Dark night rises from the sea, bells do not ring for us,
   Birds do not sing, horse does not neigh, lion and bull do not bellow,
   Dog, wolf do not howl, bear does not roar, sheep does not bleat.
6. The mistress of dark coffins [i.e., *Smert'*, "Death"] has hitherto
   taken tribute of the dead
   [dropping the unmetrical *za*],
   Hateful [reading *nenavistna*] to all living, she reigned
   cruelly in the world.
   That goddess has thrown the coffins from the graves,
   the bones from the coffins;
   Perfidious, without any pity, she has shortened
   the days of our lives.

The Judgment itself follows the Biblical description and phraseology:

12. The Judge in wrath, in fury seats himself on the throne of judgment.
    The firmament of Heaven trembles like a reed, the earth sweats.
    The condemned seeks a place, he would gladly be under the ground,
    He does not want to go to confront the enraged Judge.
13. But it is necessary for all, all appear face to face
    for this fearful scrutiny;
    The righteous take their stand near the Judge with bold heart.
    In the fastness of Hell the accused spirits tremble,
    The descendants born from Adam's flesh and blood stand up.

Christ upbraids the wicked, in terms drawn from Jesus's words in the Gospels, but enormously expanded and sharpened:

24. "I hungered, you feasted; I begged alms of you,
    But you refused me, gave me not a crust of bread.
    . . . .
25. You have worked for your belly, walking with a belly like a cask,
    You drove away the poor with a word, tired them out with labor;

135

Whatever flies, swims, walks, everything went into your belly.
Now comes the time for fasting, your belly

> has been cleansed for you.

. . . .

28. I went naked in frost, I shivered beneath your windows.
I put no clothes upon me, no one covered me with furs.
The cold rattled my teeth, my bones, you did

> not let me warm myself;

You laughed over my nakedness—you shall live in an ice-house!"

Belobotsky's third "Canto," on "Hell and the Eternal Torments,"
is the longest of the five, as has been mentioned. Dante notes
somewhere that it is part of the joys of the blest to be able to gaze
on the sufferings of those in Hell, and Belobotsky (and probably
his Latin sources) seem to anticipate this pleasure. With what can
only be described as gloating, the poet addresses the (composite
and typical) sinner:[48]

19. Why do you turn yourself, what does it profit, O man accursed?
In vain you proffer a prayer to God—you are already condemned.
Let your eye gaze downward, opened to the abyss,
Observe: this awaits you in the depth of Hell.
20. Fly headfirst, impious one, fly, law-breaker,
You won't get out from there as long as you live (!); go, sinner,
The doors are closed and bolted, you won't

> escape, you won't crawl out,

The keys have been thrown into the sea, you won't

> gnaw through your prison!

The first thirteen stanzas of Part III begin uniformly with the
phrase "Woe to . . . ," followed by a category of sinner. The list,
though doubtless not exhaustive, is inclusive enough: "Woe to the
anointed heads [of priests] " (38); "Woe to cruel masters" (39);
"Woe to the despisers of power, of kings" (40); "Woe to the
smooth faces of women" (41); "Woe to the handsome fellow, the
dandy" (42); "Woe to the miser" (43); "Woe to the vampires of
the night, that seek the lust of the flesh" (44); "Woe to the hands,
everywhere false, that have been dipped into others' goods" (45);
"Woe to those fed with the [fatted] calf" (46); "Woe to the malicious traitors, rebels and troublemakers" (47); "Woe to the
founders of evil beliefs, schismatics" (48); "Woe to the idolators"

(49); "Woe to all that have hearkened not to the commandments given by God" (50). The final strophe recapitulates:[49]

> 51. The earth befits you not, heaven will give you no aid,
>   Avaunt, disappear, God judges you, in Gehenna there
>   is no pardon for the wicked.
>   You are bound, having been condemned, hope has abandoned you.
>   Eternity, eternity without surcease has imprisoned you in Gehenna.

The beauties of Paradise fail entirely to inspire in Belobotsky the vigor and sublimity which his first three themes have elicited. The description here, not surprisingly, relies heavily on the only authentic vision of the Heavenly City which our poet is likely to have known, that of St. John the Divine (Belobotsky's knowledge of languages included Italian, but there is no indication that he had ever read Dante). After adjuring himself, evidently somewhat lost in the upper regions, "to enjoy converse with the stars," he calls on "Christ's glorious key-keeper, the apostle St. Peter," to open the heavenly gates. It is evidently something of a surprise when his appeal is heard, and he is ushered in:[50]

> 9. Glory to God, they throw open the gates on their hinges of pearl,
>   Into the court of cedar they admit [me], in the
>   eternal dwelling of the blest.
>   The magnitude of the beautiful mansions I
>   cannot observe with my eye,
>   Therefore I shall sing with joy, my soul lives for God.
> 10. Oh, a great marvel, marvel inexpressible,
>   The pavement of gold, on the walls fine [lit., "select"] gold,
>   Gates, hasps and bolts, locks being very gold,
>   Golden squares and courts, alleys and streets and promenades.
>   [21 syllables!] .

At this point it becomes necessary to enumerate the twelve precious stones which the Apocalypse mentions as the substance of the heavenly gates. It takes two complete lines to do this, with four extra syllables in the second one to accommodate the unfamiliar "chrysoprase." Whether through Belobotsky's own error or his scribe's, the beryl (*berillos*) is strangely metamorphosed into the meaningless *birimos*. Then the celestial illumination is described:[51]

137

12. On fiery horses rides the sun, the moon in a golden carriage,
   And the moon's face with horns does not visit that place
                                    [i.e., the moon is always full!]
   The Lamb of God gives light by Himself in that place,
   He emits light from His face, the heavens' eternal Sun.
13. There was no darkness there, nor night nor gloom,
   The luminary did not hide himself [there was] fullness
                                    of light from the Lamb;
   The winds made no noise, and the clouds sent down
                                    neither snow nor hail
   Nor rain nor harmful weather from themselves.

The structure of Belobotsky's poem is puzzling. For perhaps purely esthetic reasons (i.e., he did not wish to end his vision of the other world with the anticlimactic peace of Heaven!), he abandoned both his immediate sources, the "Odes" of Rader and Niess and the translation of these by Brudecki. Though originally unconnected, the two poems of Rader and two of his fellow Jesuit had been published in a single volume as *Quattuor hominis ultima* (München, 1688), and it was in this format that the Polish translator used them for his *Cztery rzeczy człowieku Ostateczne*. But Belobotsky chose to make his work a "Five Book" unit (*Pentateugum*) and accordingly finished off his eschatological vision with a selection of Jakob Balde's *De vanitate mundi* (München, 1638). The selection is small (30 out of 100 stanzas), and the theme is treated mostly by familiar *exempla*, such as the fall of Troy, the fate of "the seven wonders of the world," and the like. The grandiose spectacle of the "greatness and decline of Rome" terminates the book. The civil war between Pompey and Julius Caesar ("son-in-law and father-in-law") seems to be colored by a knowledge of Lucan's *Pharsalia*:[52]

21. From both sides arises an internecine strife of citizens;
   Neighbor pursues neighbor, there are so many instruments of war,
   Under equal banners the trumpets sound for battle,
   Regiments battle with regiments, and are
                                    shattered with the spear.
22. Son-in-law goes to encounter father-in-law, they make trial of
                                    each other with the sword,
   Ready to die for unrighteousness—but the guiltier conquers.
   Thus when honors occupy a small part of the world,
   For their proud obstinacy fields swim in blood.

138

The melancholy spectacle reaches its climax with the sack by Alaric, and the ruinous city that Belobotsky himself probably saw and which he describes most vividly:[53]

27. Terrible as were the forces of the Romans to all
          peoples, they had vanished.
 So it is when grandsons waste what fathers have laid by.
 For the heir [Polish *dziedzicowi*] of this world there
          was little tribute, plunder,
 What Nero left, Alaric carried off to the courts of the Goths.
28. Today the descendants of the Romans look for their ancient glory.
 Your gate [i.e., arch] O Trajan, the teeth of time have gnawed.
 Fallen is the seven-storied pillar of merciful Severus
          [i.e., the Septizonium]
 And Lucullus's city palace, and Titus's wall is not to be recognized.
29. No longer do tables reek with the balsam of emperor Nero,
 The hot-houses of the emperors are dirty, water
          mingled with excrement.
 In your baths, Antoninus [i.e., Caracalla], goslings paddle,
 On your plains, Tibur [Tivoli] the goats sniff the fragrant grass.
30. Shows of wonders [Pol. *dziwowisko*], councils,
          buildings, largesse of gold,
 Combats of lions with bears, various games,
 Amusing comedies, together with authors and spectators,
 Time has turned into tragedies, they all lie today beneath the feet.

The verse of Andrei Belobotsky is a kind of "purple patch" on the uniformly drab fabric of Russian seventeenth-century bookish poetry. The poet himself by his cosmopolitan background, so untypical of the Muscovite writers of the century, is an anomaly; and the lurid vigor and intensity of his poetry is altogether without parallel in Muscovy. He belongs unequivocally to the Baroque, and specifically to the Western Baroque. His affinities are with such near-contemporaries as Agrippa d'Aubigné, Andreas Gryphius and Quirinus Kuhlmann. That he wrote his *Pentateugum* in Russian rather than in German or Polish seems almost an accident; nothing about it but the language associates it with Russia. This exotic character evidently explains also the poem's neglect: there are numerous manuscripts of the works of the other syllabic poets—Belobotsky's survives in only one, and that corrupt and garbled. The Western Baroque was not very congenial to Muscovite ways of thought.

Сынъ старейши глаголе коӱцӱ

Оче моидраги бӱе любезнеиши.
азъ есмь повсадни рабъ твоӱ смиренеиши
Несмерти скоро азъ желаю тебе.
нолетъ премноги что самъ себе.
Честныа руце твои лобызаю.
честь водаати должно обѣщаю.

лӏ в̄   6

Scene from Simeon Polotsky's "The Prodigal Son,"
published in 1685.

Simeon Polotsky

Johann Gregory, 1672

CHAPTER V

SEVENTEENTH CENTURY RUSSIAN DRAMA

A. The Beginnings[1]

If the Slavic peoples had any popular mimetic genres, as they very proabably had, these remained unwritten and had no influence on the development of genuine drama, which is an entirely borrowed literary form in Russian lands. West European drama, as is well known, developed from the fusion of two traditions: a native liturgical form, fostered by the Roman Church with the aim of more vividly presenting the events of the lives of Christ and the saints than could be done by oral narrative; and the revived Graeco-Roman tradition. The Greek Orthodox church never employed drama for the same purpose as did its western rival; and Byzantine literature is almost entirely devoid of anything in dramatic form, about the only exception being the anonymous *Khristos paskhon* of the eleventh or twelfth century, a curious cento of lines from classical Greek drama made to serve the purpose of depicting Christ's death on the cross. Moreover, as has often been noted, the east Slavic peoples of the Orthodox faith experienced no such thing as a "Renaissance," and since classical Greek drama formed no part of the Byzantine ecclesiastical tradition, it remained unknown to seventeenth-century Russia. When drama made its first timid appearance in Muscovy, it was from the West that it came, not from the Greek birthplace of the dramatic genres.

The above-mentioned church drama of Christ's passion was adapted twice in the early seventeenth century by Belorussian authors: first by the printer Andrei Skulsky (1630), and later by the preacher Ioaniky Volkovich. Both of these adaptations were in

143

syllabic verse, and consisted of a series of rhetorical declamations assigned to different speakers, but with no thought of genuine dramatic performance.

As derivatives of a unique Byzantine original, the attempts by Skulsky and Volkovich could be considered as at least in the genuine East Slavic tradition; but they were isolated experiments, with no future. The drama which did soon begin to flourish in Belorussia was an imitation of Polish models, themselves derived from the Jesuit instructional drama of the West. Particularly in favor here was the allegorical type usually known in the West as "morality play," in which abstractions like "Love," "Hate," "Nature," "Conscience," etc. played parts.

During the last third of the seventeenth century two dramatic traditions, both western, took root in Muscovy and gave rise to the first genuine theater in the Russian language. Almost simultaneously the Polish Jesuit school drama was adapted for the Orthodox court of Alexei Mikhailovich by Simeon Polotsky; and German secular drama was naturalized by translations and presentations of the Lutheran pastor Johann Gottfried Gregory (d. 1675). A brief explanation of these two traditions is requisite at this point.

The Jesuit order, in its efforts to combat the spread of Protestantism, had appropriated the "school drama" of the Renaissance. This was in essence an educational device for the teaching of Latin, and was either the actual plays of Plautus, Terence or Seneca, presented by the pupils of a Latin school, or imitations of such ancient comedies and tragedies written for the purpose. Actors and audience were the students and faculties of such schools, although there was often a special festival performance to which parents and patrons might be invited. Naturally such presentations excluded all female parts. As adapted by the Jesuits the classical comedies and tragedies themselves were dropped in favor of edifying material often taken from the Bible or from the lives of saints; and as has been noted above of the Polish and Belorussian examples, there was a strong tendency to employ allegorical abstractions as "characters" in these dramas. In the West the Jesuit drama, in its efforts to compete with secular entertainment, often resorted to sumptuous costuming, music, spectacular staging and other ancillary devices, so that its effect was rather more like that of an opera than a play.

The secular drama which reached Muscovy at about the same time was German, and came in through the so-called *nemetskaia sloboda*, or "German" (i.e., foreign) settlement in the suburbs of Moscow itself. German secular drama was itself largely an offshoot of the English drama through the intermediacy of the "English players," who toured Europe giving debased versions of the great Elizabethan dramas in their native language, and thus relying heavily on action rather than words for their effects. A famous example of this development is the evolution of Christopher Marlowe's *The Tragicall History of Dr. Faustus*, through various English and German acting versions into the puppet-show which entranced the boy Goethe in the mid-eighteenth century. Since English drama did not conform, at least in the earlier Renaissance period, to the classical regulation forbidding the mixture of comic with tragic scenes in the same play, plays in this tradition in Germany usually included comic characters in order to relieve the tedium of a succession of serious episodes. A traditional comic character of this sort was named Pickelhäring; he was utilized as a buffoon in any play, irrespective of subject matter. With the Jesuit school drama the classical proprieties were maintained and the same need for relief from tragic blood and thunder was met not by the use of comic characters, but by the "interlude," a one-act short farce intruded between the acts of a serious play.

The Belorussian Simeon Polotsky has the credit of introducing the school drama into Muscovy. Taking care not to offend Orthodox sensibilities by "profane" subjects or the appearance of female characters on the stage, he took as his first theme the story of the "three youths in the fiery furnace," which was annually commemorated in a traditional ceremony in Orthodox churches. Simeon's "drama," called "On King Nebuchadnezzar, or the Golden Calf," is a very simple action employing only six characters, and closely following the Biblical story of the Book of Daniel. Departing from the school drama usage, Simeon avoids the introduction of allegorical "characters"; his persons are all flesh and blood—Nebuchadnezzar himself, his chief adviser Amir, the youths Anany, Azary and Misail, and an angel, acting as messenger.

Having broken the ice with a quasi-liturgical piece, Simeon next boldly dramatized the New Testament parable of the Prodigal Son. It is thought that his choice of subject may have been motivated by parallelism with an actual event of contemporary Muscovite history—the flight in 1660 of a son of Tsar Alexei's favorite minister, L.A. Ordyn-Nashchokin, which desolated the father. Simeon's "Prodigal Son,"[2] like its predecessor, is composed in regular syllabic verse, and was included, together with "Nebuchadnezzar," in his major verse collection, the *Ritmologion* (first printed after Simeon's death, in 1685). Again the use of allegorical abstractions is avoided, and a certain degree of realism achieved by presenting the "Son" yielding to the familiar Muscovite vices of gaming and drunkenness. Needless to say, he cannot be shown as victimized by loose women! As an example of Simeon's "Dramatic verse" may be cited the monologue of the "Son" in Part IV:

> Woe is me! Woe! What shall I do?
> I have destroyed the swine—they will kill me.
> I am dying with extreme hunger and cold,
> And I am cruelly beaten with rods.
> O how good it would be to be in my father's house,
> Rather than wander in a strange land!
> His hirelings there have bread,
> But my belly is destroyed by hunger.
> I shall go to my father, I shall bow down to his feet,
> Speaking thus, I shall make entreaty before him:
> "Father! I have sinned against heaven and toward you,
> Take me at least as your hireling,
> For I am not worthy to be called your son."
> O grant me, God, to make my way to my father!

Whether Tsar Alexei's interest in the strange, new, and absorbing western kind of entertainment was first kindled by Simeon's verse dramas is impossible to say; but certain it is that rumors of private performances, in German, in the foreign quarter came to the Tsar's ears, and he made several attempts to induce a German company to establish itself permanently in Moscow. Success in this endeavor came only in 1672, when pastor Gregory accepted the Tsar's invitation, and began to mount performances in the specially built court theater in the new palace at Preobrazhenskoe. The extant pieces which were performed by this company, and by another which followed for the short period between Gregory's death (1675) and that of the Tsar (1676) were all

146

translations or adaptations from the German, some made by Gregory himself, and following in form and tradition the "English" pattern. The subjects chosen for these dramas were all Biblical—an obvious concession to Orthodox prejudices—but the plots did not exclude female characters, and in conformity with the "English" tradition, comic scenes, sometimes rather crude, were made part of the drama itself, instead of being intruded between the acts. The first of Gregory's dramas, which has the title *Artakserksevo deistvo*, or "Artaxerxes action," is based on the book of Esther, and must have had a stunning effect on the Muscovite court, unused as it was to such spectacles, for the play employed a cast of 64 characters, was in seven acts, and lasted a full ten hours! Happily for Gregory, Tsar Alexei was utterly delighted, and other Biblical plays followed, not all of which are extant: "Tobias the Younger"; "Judith"; "The Lamentable Story of Adam and Eve"; and a "Small Entertaining Comedy of Joseph." The best of these is the "comedy" *Judith*, with a plot drawn from the apocryphal book of that name.[3] An analysis of it will be enough to give some hint of Gregory's dramaturgy. Judith, "queen" of a Jewish town, determines to rescue her people from conquest by the Assyrian general Holofernes by employing her extraordinary beauty to seduce him. She goes with her servant-girl Abra to Holofernes's tent, where he is drinking with his officers, and throws herself at his head. Holofernes, who has apparently been drinking a good deal, announces that he would like to rest a little: "Here he falls on his bed, and the others quietly retire." Abra, who is one of the play's two comic characters, misinterprets the situation, quite naturally, and asks: "Do you want me to undress you?" Judith indignantly rejects the idea and posts the girl outside the tent to prevent anyone from entering. Taking up the sword of the sleeping Holofernes, Judith addresses a prayer to the Almighty, and cuts off Holofernes's head. Holding the severed head in her hand, she goes out, and her maid inquires:

Abra. Isn't that Holofernes's head?
Judith. Why do you ask? What are you gazing at? Come speedily, let us flee.
Abra. Oh! Never would I have been so daring. Ah, what a valiant warrior's head she has cut off!... What will the poor man say, when he wakes up, and Judith has gone off with his head?

147

This is of course the center of the action, but a good deal of the interest is focused on the play's "Pickelhäring," a captive Assyrian soldier named Susakim. In a way somewhat similar to the fashion in which Spanish dramatists often employ the *gracioso* to parody the serious main action of a *comedia*, the author of *Judith* uses the buffoon Susakim to parody the "beheading" theme. Informed that he is to be executed by his Jewish captors, Susakim pleads to be allowed to "say farewell to the world," which he does of course at great length, revealing in his fond goodbyes a good deal of his own character and sordid way of life. He is finally seized by the impatient "executioners," who throw him on the ground and "with a fox's tail strike him on the neck in place of a sword, until he falls down and lies on the ground as though dead." The jokesters then run away and Susakim slowly gets up and monologizes thus:

> What I'm to do with myself now, I don't know. Am I alive or dead? Truly, I can't rightly make this out, whether I'm genuinely dead. I'm genuinely certain that I heard life retreating from me out of my inward guts into my right leg, and from my leg into my throat, and my soul exited by the right ear; only it still seems to me that I'm aware of some daylight! Here are my stockings and shoes; there lies my hat; here's my caftan and trousers—only I don't know where my head is. *(He looks everywhere for his head.)* *(To the audience)* O, you, gentlemen! If anyone of you out of love or friendship has concealed my head, I humbly beg him—without a hat—and pray him to return it to me. Or did that thief Dookh carry it off with him to his house? After this death, I'll be nothing but a ghost or an apparition; I'll go at night to Dookh's mansion, and scare him so that he will return to me my head!" *(After this he leaves the stage.)*[4]

One of the characteristics that distinguish the secular, court theater from the ecclesiastical "School drama" is the medium employed: the plays written and produced by Gregory and his successors are in prose, while the dramas of Polotsky and Dimitry Rostovsky are in syllabic verse. There is also a considerable difference in language: the foreigners who composed the court dramas were perhaps fluent in spoken Russian, but less at home with the Church Slavonic. Their efforts accordingly show a much greater—sometimes even a rather grotesque—mixture of linguistic levels than those written for the schools. Notably, however, the subjects utilized by the two dramatic systems are not markedly different:

with one exception all the court plays of the seventeenth century are on Biblical subjects. The single exception is the *Temir-aksakovo deistvo* (c. 1673), which has its rather remote ancestry in Christopher Marlowe's *Tamburlaine the Great*, by way of some German intermediaries (Temir-Aksak is the Russian—really Turkish—name: "Timur the Lame").

Another distinguishing characteristic is, as we have seen, the unabashed use of comedy scenes in the court plays. In keeping with the Jesuit tradition and Ukrainian and Belorussian usages, the earlier school plays were entirely serious, and the audience's need for relaxation after the endless declamations was granted a slight concession by the "interludes," one-act skits intruded between the acts of the serious work.[5]

Interpenetration of the two systems was inevitable, and one of the first evidences of this is to be found in the school dramas of Dmitry Tuptalo, metropolitan of Rostov. Dmitry "Rostovsky," already well known as a poet and as author of the very popular and highly dramatic collection of saints' lives, the *Chet'ii Minei*, composed especially for his students in the monastery school which he founded in Rostov, a number of dramas on Biblical subjects.[6] The parts in these were played by the students, and the audience was of students, and probably a few secular patrons. It is not surprising therefore that the dramas "Birth of Christ" *(Rozhdestvo Khristovo)*, "Resurrection of Christ" *(Voskreseniie Khristovo)*, "Ascension of the Virgin" *(Uspenskaia drama)*, etc., should be didactic in tone, with long, rhetorical tirades pronounced often by such allegorical figures as "Love," "Death," "Hell," and the like. What is surprising is that Dmitry boldly and in defiance of tradition introduces comic characters and scenes into these serious situations. A typical example is afforded by the quite realistic shepherds of the Christmas play[7]—genuine Russians all, the simple-minded old Boris, the one-eyed and hunchbacked Avram, and the smart young Afonia. As they regale themselves with bread and vodka they hear music, and it is some while before they realize that this is not the singing of small children or little birds, but of the heavenly host! The realism is of course rudimentary, and the humor not particularly subtle, but these ingredients are novel enough in seventeenth-century Russian verse to deserve mention. An analogy with the "Second Shepherds' Play" of the English "Wakefield Cycle" comes of course to mind.

B. The "Tragicomedy of Vladimir" of Feofan Prokopovich

Dmitry Rostovsky's school plays belong to the years 1702-06. In the year 1705 another school drama was written and produced which marks an epoch in Russian literary history. On the occasion of the annual school celebration of the Mogila Academy of Kiev for the year 1705 the young professor of oratory of the Academy, Feofan Prokopovich, nephew of the Academy's rector, produced his five-act *Tragicomedy of St. Vladimir*.[8] Prokopovich had studied for four years in Poland and in Rome, chiefly in Jesuit schools. Upon his appointment to the faculty of the Academy in Kiev he gave a course of lectures in 1705 on "the art of poetry," which were published as a text some fifty years after the author's death.[9] The *Tragicomedy* was an exemplification of the rules and recommendations of these lectures. According to Feofan:[10]

> . . . tragedy is poetry which imitates the important actions of illustrious men, and particularly their changes of fortune and calamities, by means of the action and speech of the characters. Comedy, however, is poetry which sets forth the public and private acts of common people with the purpose of giving instruction for life and above all of reprehending the evil manners of men—this likewise both by action and speech of the characters, together with jests and witticisms. From these a third mixed kind is constituted, which is called tragicomedy. . . . since in it laughable and humorous things are mingled with serious and lamentable ones, and common with illustrious characters.

In another well-known school text of the period[11] we read: "The tragicomedy is a certain mixture of comedy and tragedy, so that, despite the rules of comedy, it introduces more noble and lofty personages; and in distinction from tragedy the tragicomedy always ends with a happy outcome."

Rostovsky's plays were short ones, seldom exceeding two acts, and sometimes with no indicated division at all. *St. Vladimir* is the first Russian example of the five-act drama, in verse, with a limited cast, and conforming to the "unities" of time and place, such as had become the classical usage in the West. In one respect, however—that of treating the eminently serious subject of the conversion to Christianity of Grand Duke Vladimir of Kiev (988 A.D.)—in a "tragicomedy" Feofan is highly unconventional. In this respect *St. Vladimir* seems to follow the same innovative line as Dmitry Rostovsky in his school plays.

The plot of *The Tragicomedy of St. Vladimir* is extremely simple. The exposition is given by a sort of prologue, in which the ghost of Yaropolk, Prince Vladimir's murdered brother, appears to the high priest Zherivol. Yaropolk's spirit complains bitterly of his brother's unfraternal conduct (Vladimir had murdered him and seized his wife and throne), and warns Zherivol that the man who has behaved thus towards his own brother is now about to commit an even greater crime—the destruction of the very gods themselves! Vladimir is contemplating conversion to Christianity. Zherivol promises to obtain the aid of the spirits of Hell to prevent this enterprise. The second act begins the "complication" of the plot: the priest Kuroyad (whose name means "Chicken-Eater"—Zherivol means "Bull-Devourer") proclaims the great festival of the god Perun. He is interrupted in his proclamation by the third priest, Piar (whose name means "Drinker"), who bids him halt proceedings because the high priest is not ready; Piar has seen him in the wilderness communing with the evil spirits. Zherivol then enters, lamenting, and announces Vladimir's terrible intentions. He thereupon performs his incantations and the first two hellish spirits appear, the Demon of the World and the Demon of Censure (i.e., the personifications of worldly ambition and of critical rationalism). Last comes the Demon of the Flesh (a female), which the priests expect to be particularly effective against Vladimir, with his three hundred wives! The third act introduces the hero himself for the first time: Vladimir converses with his two sons Boris and Gleb (the later sainted martyrs) about the message brought by the "philosopher" (i.e., theologian) sent by the Emperor

151

of Constantinople. This colloquy is interrupted by the appearance of Zherivol with the pathetic announcement that the gods are in a very bad way—they are starving because of the cessation of sacrifices! Vladimir sends for the "philosopher," and orders the representatives of the two religions to stage a debate. Zherivol is ignominiously worsted and dismissed, after which the Christian explains the principal items of his faith, ending with the threatening picture of the Last Judgment. The denouement of the drama comes, as usual, in the fourth act. Vladimir dismisses his two sons and is subjected to the successive temptations of the Demons of the World, of Censure, and of the Flesh. He wavers, but is of course victorious in the end. The three Demons, forming a chorus, make a last struggle against his constancy, but finally leave with threats of vengeance. The fifth act forms as it were the epilogue, showing the consequences of the conversion of Vladimir. Kuroyad and Piar mourn the downfall of the gods, the sickness of Zherivol, and their own hunger. The Prince's general Mechislav ("Famous with the Sword") denounces them as traitors because they have not carried out the prince's orders to destroy all idols. The priests try to evade the charge by the pretense of not having heard the orders, but are taken into custody, while the soldiers break up the idols which are on the stage. The officer Khrabry ("Valiant"), performing the office of the classical "Messenger," recounts to his superior the impressive scene of Vladimir's baptism. A courier enters with the gift of a sword to the general from "Prince Vasily" —Vladimir's new name assumed at baptism. The drama ends with the appearance of the apostle St. Andrew (traditionally supposed to have visited Kiev and prophesied Russia's conversion) with a host of angels. St. Andrew forecasts various events of subsequent Russian history, ending with a glorification of Ivan Mazeppa, hetman of the Ukraine, and patron of the Academy where the drama is being given.

It will be seen from this summary that even though the "action" is extremely sketchy, and consists almost entirely of declamation, there is considerable opportunity for spectacle—the two choruses, consisting of the Demons, and of St. Andrew supported by the heavenly host; and the demolition of the pagan idols before the eyes of the spectators. The influence of Seneca, by way of the seventeenth-century Jesuit drama, is apparent in the apparition of Yaropolk's ghost, and in the extremely lengthy and rhetorical speeches. Thus, the fourth scene of the third act consists of some 175 lines by the "philosopher," interrupted only briefly by Vladimir's questions. The longest single tirade is one of 93 lines. It is of course not surprising that it should take this length of time to expound all the major articles of the Christian creed, and to an audience composed of the students and faculty of an ecclesiastical seminary such an exposition may have had considerable interest; but the interest can scarcely be considered dramatic.

The liveliest portions of the drama are without question those that involve the comic characters. The three priests are caricatures, the principal features of their personalities being indicated by their names. When Piar halts Kuroyad's proclamation of the great festival of Perun with the announcement that Zherivol is not ready, Kuroyad expresses his disbelief as follows:[12]

> This is an unseemly speech. He hasn't time to sacrifice? You are being lied to, friend, and you believe it. I do not. I think he would have liked to have one continuous festival. I shall tell you a marvelous thing: I have seen him, when having fed on numerous sacrifices, he lay in the cold, and his belly was like a huge storehouse. However, even in such satiety, he gave signs of hunger and great greed: he gnashed with his teeth, and for a long time moved his mouth and throat without measure. And is your word, Piar, "He doesn't have time," deserving of belief? Even in his sleep Zherivol devours.

At the beginning of Act V, when Vladimir has already made his decision and the pagan sacrifices have come to an end, "Chicken-Eater" moans:

> I want something to eat, to eat! Alack, to eat! I want to eat! Woe is me! Ruin has come.

Piar protests:

> This evil is still but small.
> *Kur.* You call it but a small evil to waste away with hunger? And what is more, honored priests and truth-telling sacrificers through the whole world! But look, I went to the village to *buy* chickens! That this time should come!

When Piar hints that after all the worst aspect of the famine is the

153

plight of the gods, Kuroyad hastily assures him:[13]

> No, friend! I do not grieve for myself, I grieve for the gods. For if
> sacrifices are cut off, I can buy meat, but a god does not have money
> and cannot go to the village; therefore death is prepared for us—I mean
> for him. And this makes me doubly sorrowful.

Zherivol's "debate" with the "philosopher" is farcical; one of
his most telling points is the query: "But tell me, what delight in
food does your god chiefly seek for? What does he like best to
eat? Tell, I pray you." To this the philosopher contemptuously
replies: "If you were not so earthy, you would be able to realize
that a humble spirit is the favorite sacrifice of God." This is too
much for Zherivol and his followers, who burst out laughing:[14]

> Ha, ha, ha, ha! Hear this! Hear about the famous Christian god! Then
> he doesn't even drink—thirsty, hungry and miserable—a spirit suffices
> him—he is sated with vapor!

One aspect of the drama remains to be mentioned—the political one. There can be no doubt that the audience of 1705 saw, and
were meant to see, behind the figure of Prince Vladimir the for-
midable image of Peter the Great, and behind the ridiculous and
contemptible opponents of the Prince the "Old Muscovite" party
who regarded Peter's reforms with pious horror. That the point of
the satire did not escape its victims is evidenced by the wording
of a denunciation of Prokopovich made in 1716 when he was a
candidate for a bishopric: "He calls the Orthodox archpriests and
priests 'sacrificers' [zhretsami] and Pharisees; Russian clergymen
he calls 'bull-devourers' [zherivolami], hypocrites, idolatrous sacrificers."[15]

The Tragicomedy of St. Vladimir marks a turning point
in the history of the Russian drama. Earlier examples of the dramatic genres are crude, tentative, derivative and insignificant from a
literary point of view except as indications of later possibilities.
Feofan's drama, awkward and imperfect though it may be, has
elements in it of genuine drama, such as the eighteenth century
will make full use of. The inner debate in the soul of Vladimir in
Act IV, externalized by the use of the chorus of Demons, is a
direct, and not altogether unworthy, predecessor of the great

154

psychological debates which make up so much of the "action" of Sumarokov's tragedies. It can hardly, of course, be compared seriously with such great psychological triumphs as Phaedra's agonized conflict with herself or Titus's and Berenice's stern self-renunciations, but it is of the same kind.

The language of the drama is, inevitably, one of its weakest aspects. It is a somewhat Ukrainianized form of the common Church Slavonic, remote from spoken Russian. The verse form employed in the dialogue is the usual 13-syllable line, which Kantemir was to label the Russian "heroic verse," with couplet rhyme. Certain portions of the play, however, such as Kuroyad's proclamation at the beginning of Act II, Zherivol's song of incantation in the third scene of the same act, and the long lyric "chorus" of Prelest (i.e., the Demon of the Flesh in the guise presumably of Venus) in Act IV are composed in other syllabic meters. The song of Prelest is metrically very complex, with sections (*not* strophic) of short lines of five or seven syllables alternating with long lines of thirteen, and with occasional enclosing rhymes, as well as the customary couplets. An approximation of the effect of Feofan's lyric verse may be obtained from this version of Zherivol's incantation:[16]

> Rise to aid us, hellish regions,
> Send us speedily your legions,
> Move your strength, your power appalling—
> For, behold, your honor's falling.
>
> Winged wind that on the ocean
> Sets the ship in speedy motion,
> Bring to us with hurried pinions
> Helpful power of Hell's dominions.
>
> Fly, O spirits, fly and carry
> Aid to us, and do not tarry!
> Whet the sting of wrath unending:
> Cruel the time on us descending.

Feofan Prokopovich did not follow up his success with *St. Vladimir* by composing again in the dramatic genre. In fact, his subsequent career was so thoroughly involved with politics that it left him little time for literary activity. Summoned to St.

Petersburg in 1716, after having through Peter's favor served in rapid succession as professor of philosophy, prefect, and rector of the Mogila Academy and abbot of the Bratsky Monastery, he was consecrated to a provincial bishopric despite the opposition of his enemies. He became shortly one of Peter's most trusted assistants, and when Stefan Yavorsky, the president of the Holy Synod, showed himself opposed to Peter's church reforms, Feofan was appointed assistant director of the Synod and in effect put over the head of his titular superior. It was Prokopovich who composed the "Spiritual Regulation" which Peter promulgated in 1720-21, and who helped the Tsar suppress his rebellious son Alexei. In 1720 Feofan was created Archbishop of Novgorod. His activity after the death of Peter the Great (1725) had best be considered later.

The Lopukhin Tower and Church of the Transfiguration in Moscow's Novodevichi Monastery, 1687-89.

*"They are coming" ("Muscovites watch the entry of a
foreign embassy into Moscow at the end of the 17th century"),
Oil painting by Andrei Ryabushkin, 1901.*

CONCLUSION

A reader looking for a body of exciting and attractive litera-ture in Russia's seventeenth century will be disappointed. Even the pieces that stand out most conspicuously—Avvakum's "Autobiog-raphy," "The Tale of Sorrow-Misfortune," and "Frol Skobeev"—cannot be appreciated as literature independently, but require a great deal of elucidation before their genuine qualities become evident. Particularly disappointing is the verse of the age, very lit-tle of which rises above a drearily pedestrian level. The drama is infantile. If the century as a whole is compared with the same period of time in western Europe, where Shakespeare, Jonson, Donne and Milton; Corneille, Racine, Molière and La Fontaine; Góngora, Tirso de Molina, Cervantes and Calderón were writing masterpieces that stand among the greatest achievements of the human spirit, Russia's contribution must look pitiably scant and insignificant.

It must nevertheless, be reckoned with as indispensable in the development of a literature that blossoms in another century and a half in the works of Pushkin and Lermontov, Turgenev, Gon-charov, Dostoevsky and Tolstoi. It is the seventeenth century that breaks at last the long medieval domination of literature by the church, as laymen of the gentry and merchant classes begin to write. In the seventeenth century for the first time the anonymity of literary composition begins to disappear, and individual names and personalities emerge from a formerly homogeneous mass of writing governed only by the conventions of the genre. A dis-tinctively court literature comes into being for the first time, which will dominate the following century and be definitively dis-carded only in the nineteenth. Linguistically the seventeenth cen-tury is most significant for the first still tentative attempts to utilize the native Russian language as a literary medium instead of the obsolescent and alien Russo-Slavonic of the church. The mur-ky and lumbering verse of Medvedev and Belobotsky shows a glimmer of the poetical potentialities of the evolving language which Lomonosov and Derzhavin in the next century were to realize in part, and Pushkin, Baratynsky, Tyutchev and Lermontov most fully in the romantic period. The naive and unpremeditated naturalism of both style and vocabulary, the use of a vigorous and colloquial Russian in Avvakum's *Autobiography* leads directly to such monuments of proto-realism as Fonvizin's *The Minor* or Kapnist's *Iabeda*, and from them to Griboedov and *Eugene Onegin*. The clumsy and incoherent psychology which the unknown author of the "Tale of Sorrow-Misfortune" gives his young "hero" may seem a far cry from even such a credibly human portrait as that of Chulkov's "comely cook," and worlds removed from such a masterpiece of characterization as that of Dostoevsky's "underground man"; yet it is indubitably a first faltering step in that direction.

Seventeenth-century Russian literature has little of independent value to offer and need not long detain the impatient student. But the germs of the whole great flowering of Russia's literature in the eighteenth, nineteenth and twentieth centuries are in it, and it is ignored at one's peril. After all, even the most childish and absurd *juvenilia* of a great poet, e.g. Tyutchev or Rilke, will reveal to the discerning eye the direction that will lead to his mature triumphs. *Ex ungue leonem*—the seventeenth-century claw of the Russian beast may be a small and feeble one, but it is still a lion's.

"St. George and the Dragon," 17th-century Vologda icon

*St. Basil's Cathedral and the "Lobnoe mesto" (proclamation spot), from
Olearius's journey of 1636.*

NOTES / BIBLIOGRAPHY / INDEX

SOURCE TITLES AND ABBREVIATIONS USED IN THE NOTES

GENERAL WORKS ON SEVENTEENTH-CENTURY RUSSIAN LITERATURE

Gudzy, N.K. ISTORIIA DREVNEI RUSSKOI LITERATURY. M.: Uchpedgiz, 1941. [GUDZY: ISTORIIA]
HISTORY OF EARLY RUSSIAN LITERATURE, tr. Susan Wilbur Jones, intro. Gleb Struve. New York: Macmillan, 1949. [GUDZY: HISTORY]
Gukovsky, G.A. RUSSKAIA LITERATURA XVIII VEKA. M.: Uchpedgiz, 1939. [GUKOVSKY]
ISSLEDOVANIIA I MATERIALY PO DREVNERUSSKOI LITERATURE. M.: AN, 1961. [ISSLEDOVANIIA]
ISTORIIA RUSSKOI LITERATURY: T. II, ch. ii. M.: AN, 1949; T. III. M. 1941. [IRL]
ISTORIIA RUSSKOI POEZII V DVUKH TOMAKH. L.: "Nauka," 1968. [IRP]
ISTORIIA ZHANROV V RUSSKOI LITERATURE X-XVII VEKOV. L. 1972. [IZH]
Likhachev, D.S. POETIKA DREVNERUSSKOI LITERATURY. L. 1967. [POETIKA]
Likhachev, D.S. RAZVITIE RUSSKOI LITERATURY X-XVII VEKOV. L. 1973. [RAZVITIE]
Likhachev, D.S. Velikoe nasledie. M.: "Sovremennik," 1975. [NASLEDIE]
Panchenko, A.M. RUSSKAIA STIKHOTVORNAIA KUL'TURA XVII VEKA. L. 1973. [PANCHENKO]
RUSSKII FOL'KLOR: T. XIII, RUSSKAIA NARODNAIA PROZA. L. 1972. [FOL'K-LOR]
RUSSKAIA LITERATURA NA RUBEZHE DVUKH EPOKH (XVII-NACHALO XVIII V.). Ed. A.N. Robinson. M.: "Nauka," 1971. [ROBINSON]
XVII VEK V MIROVOM LITERATURNOM RAZVITII. M. 1969. [XVII VEK]
Stender-Petersen, Adolf. GESCHICHTE DER RUSSISCHEN LITERATUR. München: Beck, 1957. Vol. I. [STENDER-PETERSEN]
Vodovozov, N.V. ISTORIIA DREVNEI RUSSKOI LITERATURY. M. 1962. [VODO-VOZOV]

ANTHOLOGIES AND COLLECTIVE WORKS

Gudzy, N.K. KHRESTOMATIIA PO DREVNEI RUSSKOI LITERATURE XI-XVII VEKOV. M. 1947. [GUDZY: KHRESTOMATIIA]
KHRESTOMATIIA PO ISTORII RUSSKOGO IAZYKA: CHAST' VTORAIA, VYPUSK PERVYI. Ed. S.P. Obnorsky and S.G. Barkhudarov. M. 1949. [OBNOR.]
KHRESTOMATIIA PO ISTORII SSSR: T. I, S DREVNEISHIKH VREMEN DO KON-TSA XVII VEKA. Ed. V.I. Lebedev, M.N. Tikhomirov, V.E. Syroechkovsky. M. 1949. [LEBEDEV]
KHRESTOMATIIA PO ISTORII SSSR XVI-XVII VV. Ed. A.A. Zimin. M. 1962. [ZI-MIN]
KHRESTOMATIIA PO RUSSKOI LITERATURE XVIII VEKA. Ed. A.V. Kokorev. M. 1961. [KOKOREV]
Manning, Clarence A. ANTHOLOGY OF EIGHTEENTH-CENTURY RUSSIAN LITER-ATURE. New York: King's Crown Press, 1951. [MANNING] Vol. I.
RUSSKAIA DEMOKRATICHESKAIA POEZIIA XVII VEKA. Ed. V.P. Adrianova-Peretts and D.S. Likhachev. M.-L.: "Sovetskii Pisatel'," Biblioteka Poeta. Bol'-shaia seriia, 1962. [DEMOKRAT.]
RUSSKAIA SILLABICHESKAIA POEZIIA XVII-XVIII VV. Ed. A.M. Panchenko. L.: "Sovetskii Pisatel'," Biblioteka poeta. Bol'shaia seriia, 1970. [SILLABICHES-KAIA POEZIIA]
Stender-Petersen, Adolf. ANTHOLOGY OF OLD RUSSIAN LITERATURE. New York: Columbia University Press, 1954. [OLD RUSS.]
Zenkovsky, Serge A. MEDIEVAL RUSSIA'S EPICS, CHRONICLES AND TALES. New York: Dutton, 1963. [ZENKOVSKY]

NOTES

Abbreviated titles refer to works listed on p. 165.

CHAPTER I
1. POETIKA, p. 20.
2. D.S. Likhachev, XVII VEK V RUSSKOI LITERATURE; in XVII VEK, p. 324.
3. Ibid., 304-18.
4. PANCHENKO, p. 3.
5. SKAZANIE AVRAAMIIA PALITSYNA, ed. L.V. Cherepin (M.-L. 1955).
6. RUSSKAIA ISTORICHESKAIA BIBLIOTEKA, T. XIII, pp. 479-83. See also LEBEDEV, pp. 357-58. Revised version, SKAZANIE, pp. 105-06.
7. SKAZANIE, pp. 229-30.
8. VODOVOZOV, pp. 277-81. See also ZIMIN, pp. 254-63.
9. GUDZY: KHRESTOMATIIA, pp. 297-99. See also OLD RUSS., pp. 317-25.
10. GUDZY: KHRESTOMATIIA, pp. 299-313. See also OLD RUSS., pp. 325-42.
11. VODOVOZOV, pp. 307-12.
12. ZIMIN, pp. 245-46.
13. GUDZY: KHRESTOMATIIA, p. 300.
14. Ibid., 311.
15. Ibid., 312.
16. SILLABICHESKAIA POEZIIA, p. 13.
17. Ibid., 72.
18. GUDZY: KHRESTOMATIIA, pp. 313-20; OLD RUSS., pp. 342-51.
19. GUDZY: KHRESTOMATIIA, pp. 415-19.
20. Ibid., 419.
21. Ibid., 419-25.
22. Ibid., 424.
23. OBNOR., p. 30.
24. Ibid., 31-33.
25. POETIKA, pp. 94, 98.
26. GUDZY: KHRESTOMATIIA, pp. 320-26; OLD RUSS., pp. 380-87.
27. OLD RUSS., pp. 387-484.
28. L.A. Dmitriev, ZHANR SEVERNORUSSKIKH ZHITII; in IZH, pp. 181-202.
29. Ibid., 193.
30. Ibid., 194.

CHAPTER II
1. D.S. Likhachev, XVII VEK V RUSSKOI LITERATURE; in XVII VEK, pp. 320-24.
2. RAZVITIE, pp. 172-83 (VELIKIE STILI I STIL' BAROKKO).
3. GUDZY: KHRESTOMATIIA, pp. 357-71. See also V.F. Rzhiga, POVEST' O SAVVE GRUDTSYNE, in ISSLEDOVANIIA, pp. 313-25; and OLD RUSS., pp. 437-53.
4. GUDZY: KHRESTOMATIIA, pp. 390-97. See also NASLEDIE, pp. 288-99.
5. GUDZY: KHRESTOMATIIA, pp. 426-38. See also V.D. Kuz'mina, RUSSKAIA SKAZKA O BOVE KOROLEVICHE V LUBOCHNYKH IZDANIIAKH XVII-XX VEKA, in ISSLEDOVANIIA, pp. 148-92.
6. GUDZY: KHRESTOMATIIA, pp. 439-50. See also L.N. Pushkarev, POVEST' O ERUSLANE LAZAREVICHE V RUSSKOI LUBOCHNOI KARTINKE XIX-NACHA-LA XX VEKA, in ROBINSON, pp. 351-70.
7. GUDZY: KHRESTOMATIIA, pp. 371-80. See also OLD RUSS., pp. 460-70.
8. GUDZY: KHRESTOMATIIA, pp. 402-05. See also V.V. Mitrofanova, "Narodnaia skazka o Ershe i rukopisnaia povest' o Ershe Ershoviche," in FOL'KLOR, pp. 166-78.
9. DEMOKRAT, p. 15.
10. GUDZY: KHRESTOMATIIA, pp. 406-10.
11. GUDZY: HISTORY, pp. 492-97.
12. GUDZY: KHRESTOMATIIA, pp. 399-402.
13. Ibid., 397-99.
14. GUDZY: HISTORY, pp. 484-86.
15. Ibid., pp. 486-87. See also GUDZY: KHRESTOMATIIA, pp. 405-06.
16. ZHITIE PROTOPOPA AVVAKUMA IM SAMIM NAPISANNOE I DRUGIE EGO SOCHINENIIA. Ed. N.K. Gudzy. Intro. V.E. Gusev (M. 1960). See also A.S. Demin, "Real'no-bytovye detali v zhitii protopopa Avvakuma," in ROBINSON, pp. 230-46; and NASLEDIE, pp. 299-312.

167

17. ZHITIE, p. 71; ZENKOVSKY, p. 335.
18. ZHITIE, p. 35.
19. ZHITIE, p. 78; ZENKOVSKY, pp. 342-43.
20. ZHITIE, p. 109; ZENKOVSKY, p. 369.
21. ZHITIE, p. 108; ZENKOVSKY, p. 368.
22. ZHITIE, p. 63.
23. Ibid., 78.
24. ZHITIE, p. 87; ZENKOVSKY, p. 351.
25. IRL, Vol. II, Part ii: ZHITIE EPIFANIIA (I.P. Eremin), pp. 322-26; A.N. Robinson, AVTOBIOGRAFIIA EPIFANIIA, in ISSLEDOVANIIA, pp. 101-32. See also S.A. Zenkovsky, DER MOENCH EPIFANIJ UND DIE ENTSTEHUNG DER ALTRUSSISCHEN AUTOBIOGRAPHIE, in DIE WELT DER SLAVEN, Jahrgang I, H. 3 (Wiesbaden, 1956), pp. 256-92.

CHAPTER III
1. VODOVOZOV, pp. 284-86. See also ZIMIN, pp. 267-69.
2. RUSSKIE NARODNYI EPOS; SVODNYI TEKST. Ed. N.V. Vodovozov. Afterword S.K. Shambinago (M. 1947). See also IRP, pp. 13-25 (L.E. Emel'ianov), and DEMOK., pp. 17-20.
3. BYLINY V ZAPISIAKH I PERESKAZAKH XVII-XVIII VEKOV (M.-L.: AN, 1960), pp. 219-28. See also DEMOK.
4. DEMOK., pp. 23-25.
5. GUDZY: ISTORIIA, p. 446.
6. Ibid., 445.
7. DEMOK., p. 21.
8. OBNOR., pp. 7-14.
9. Ibid., 9.
10. Text in GUDZY: KHRESTOMATIIA, pp. 342-53 and in OLD RUSS., pp. 425-36. See also NASLEDIE, pp. 312-32.
11. NASLEDIE, p. 330.

CHAPTER IV
1. RUSSKAIA SILLABICHESKAIA POEZIIA XVII-XVIII VV. and RUSSKAIA STIKHOTVORNAIA KUL'TURA XVII VEKA [SILLABICHESKAIA POEZIIA and PANCHENKO].
2. SANCTI ROMANI MELODI CANTICA, ed. Maas and C.A. Trypanis (Oxford, 1963), p. 196: "On the Resurrection III."
3. G.M. Prokhorov, "K istorii liturgicheskoi poezii: gimny i molitvy patriarkha Filofei Kokkina," in IZH, p. 135.
4. V.N. Peretts, ISTORIKO-LITERATURNYE ISSLEDOVANIIA I MATERIALY, Vol. III (St. P., 1902), pp. 14-15; quoted in SILLABICHESKAIA POEZIIA, pp. 11-12.
5. SILLABICHESKAIA POEZIIA, pp. 43-55.
6. Ibid., 37-40.
7. Ibid., 56-59.
8. Ibid., 60-70. See also Sergei Zenkovsky, "Drug Samozvantsa. Eretik i stikhotvorets (Kniaz' Ivan Andreevich Khvorostinin)," OPYTY, Vol. VI (New York, 1956), pp. 77-88.
9. PANCHENKO, pp. 34-77. See also SILLABICHESKAIA POEZIIA, pp. 73-95.
10. PANCHENKO, p. 39.
11. Ibid., 55.
12. Ibid., 103-15. See also SILLABICHESKAIA POEZIIA, pp. 96-103.
13. SILLABICHESKAIA POEZIIA, pp. 99-100.
14. Ibid., 104-73.
15. Ibid., 216-49. See also A. Kh. Gorfunkel', "Andrei Belobotskii—poet i filosof kontsa XVII-nachala XVIII v," in TRUDY OTDELA DREVNERUSSKOI LITERATURY INSTITUTA RUSSKOI LITERATURY (PUSHKINSKOGO DOMA AKADEMII NAUK SSSR) [TODRL] (M.-L. 1962), Vol. XVIII, pp. 188-213; and A. Kh. Gorfunkel', " 'Penteteugum' Andreia Belobotskogo (iz istorii pol'sko-russkikh literaturnykh sviazei)," TODRL, Vol. XXI (M.-L. 1965), pp. 39-64.
16. Gorfunkel', TODRL, Vol. XXI, pp. 39-40.
17. SILLABICHESKAIA POEZIIA, pp. 250-54.
18. Ibid., 255-65.
19. Ibid., 104-73.
20. Ibid., 108-11.

21. MANNING, pp. 9-10.
22. SILLABICHESKAIA POEZIIA, pp. 115-67.
23. Ibid., 130.
24. Ibid., 121.
25. Ibid., 153.
26. Ibid., 111-15.
27. Ibid., 184-203. See also E.V. Kolosova, " 'Sozertsanie kratkoe' Sil'vestra Medvedeva i traditsii russkoi istoricheskoi povesti v XVII veke," in ROBINSON, pp. 207-29.
28. SILLABICHESKAIA POEZIIA, pp. 188-90.
29. Ibid., 190-91.
30. Ibid., 196-99.
31. Ibid., 203-15.
32. Ibid., 203.
33. DOMOSTROI PO KONSHINSKOMU SPISKU I PODOBNYM, K IZDANIIU PRIGOTOVIL A. ORLOV (M. 1908).
34. SILLABICHESKAIA POEZIIA, p. 206.
35. PANCHENKO, p. 196.
36. SILLABICHESKAIA POEZIIA, p. 213.
37. PANCHENKO, p. 196.
38. SILLABICHESKAIA POEZIIA, pp. 213-14.
39. Ibid., 250-54.
40. Ibid., 253.
41. Ibid., 255-65.
42. PANCHENKO, pp. 140-41.
43. SILLABICHESKAIA POEZIIA, pp. 262-64.
44. Ibid., pp. 216-49. See also Gorfunkel', TODRL XVIII, pp. 188-213 and TODRL XXI, pp. 39-64.
45. TODRL XXI, pp. 39-64.
46. SILLABICHESKAIA POEZIIA, pp. 218-20.
47. Ibid., 223-24.
48. Ibid., 234.
49. Ibid., 239.
50. Ibid., 241-42.
51. Ibid., 242.
52. Ibid., 247-48.
53. Ibid., 248-49.

CHAPTER V

1. GUDZY: HISTORY, pp. 515-29. See also STENDER-PETERSEN, pp. 276-96.
2. GUDZY: KHRESTOMATIIA, pp. 486-93.
3. Ibid., 477-86.
4. Ibid., 483.
5. Two interludes are printed in GUDZY: KHRESTOMATIIA, pp. 491-96; one in MANNING, pp. 18-19, and three in KOKOREV, pp. 45-49.
6. Rostovsky's two-act drama VENETS DIMITRIU, on the martyrdom of St. Demetrius, is printed in the collection RANNIAIA RUSSKAIA DRAMATURGIIA (XVII-PERVAIA POLOVINA XVIII V.), Vol. 4: P'ESY STOLICHNYKH I PROVINTSIAL'NYKH TEATROV PERVOI POLOVINY XVIII V. (M.: AN, 1975), pp. 49-92.
7. OBNOR., pp. 61-65.
8. Feofan Prokopovich, SOCHINENIIA, ed. I.P. Eremin (M.-L. 1961), pp. 147-206.
9. Ibid., 229-33.
10. Liber II, caput x: Ibid., 313.
11. IRL, Vol. III: LITERATURA XVIII VEKA, CHAST' PERVAIA, p. 108 (I.P. Eremin).
12. Feofan Prokopovich, p. 167.
13. Ibid., 194-95.
14. Ibid., 180.
15. GUKOVSKY, p. 17.
16. Feofan Prokopovich, p. 166.

ABBREVIATIONS

(These are the standard abbreviations listed in the latest MLA International
  Bibliography.)

Aatseel	American Association of Teachers of Slavic and East European Languages
AR	Antioch Review
AUMLA	Journal of Australasian Universities Language and Literature Association
BNYPL	Bulletin of the New York Public Library
CASS	Canadian-American Slavic Studies [Formerly *CSS*]
CL	Comparative Literature
CLS	Comparative Literature Studies (U. of Ill.)
CSP	Canadian Slavonic Papers
CSS	Canadian Slavic Studies [Now *CASS*]
DA	Dissertation Abstracts
DAI	Dissertation Abstracts International [Supersedes *DA*]
ECLife	Eighteenth-Century Life
ECS	Eighteenth-Century Studies (U. of Cal., Davis)
ESl	Études slaves et est-Européennes
FI	Forum Italicum
FMLS	Forum for Modern Language Studies (U. of St. Andrews, Scotland)
GR	Germanic Review
GSlav	Germano-Slavica
HSS	Harvard Slavic Studies
IJSLP	International Journal of Slavic Linguistics and Poetics
ISS	Indiana Slavic Studies
JES	Journal of European Studies
JHI	Journal of the History of Ideas
M&L	Music and Letters (London)
MelbSS	Melbourne Slavonic Studies
MLR	Modern Language Review
MusQ	Musical Quarterly
NZSJ	New Zealand Slavonic Journal
OL	Orbis Litterarum
OPLLL	Occasional Papers in Language, Literature, and Linguistics (Ohio U.)
OSP	Oxford Slavonic Papers

PMLA	Publications of the Modern Language Association of America
PPNCFL	Proceedings of the Pacific Northwest Conference on Foreign Languages
RLC	Revue de Littérature Comparée
RLT	Russian Literature Triquarterly
RusL	Russian Literature
RusR	Russian Review
SB	Studies in Bibliography: Papers of the Bibliographical Society of the University of Virginia
SCB	South Central Bulletin
SEEJ	Slavic and East European Journal
SEER	Slavic and East European Review
SGECRN	Study Group of Eighteenth-Century Russia Newsletter
SlavR	Slavic Review (Seattle)
SPR	Slavistic Printings and Reprintings
SR	Sewanee Review
SSl	Scando-Slavica (Copenhagen)
SVEC	Studies on Voltaire and the Eighteenth Century
Thr	Theatre Research/Recherches Theatrales
YWMLS	Year's Work in Modern Language Studies

BIBLIOGRAPHY

RUSSIAN LITERATURE OF THE SEVENTEENTH CENTURY

Alexander, Alex. E. *Bylina and Fairy Tale: The Origins of Russian Heroic Poetry.* (SPR 281). The Hague: Mouton, 1973. 162 pp.

Andreyev, N. "Russian Studies: Literature, from the Beginning to 1700." *YWMLS* 27 (for 1965): 636-40; 28 (for 1966): 668-73; 29 (for 1967): 627-31; 30 (for 1968): 726-33; 31 (for 1969): 770-82; 32 (for 1970): 762-73; 33 (for 1971): 828-37; 36 (covers 1973-74): 833-43.

Arbatsky, Yury G. "Traits of Humanitas Heroica in the Extreme North of the U.S.S.R." *ESl* 7:93-7.

Avvakum, Archpriest. Translations in Wiener and Zenkovsky.

Cant, Catherine B.H. "The Archpriest Avvakum and His Scottish Contemporaries." *SEER* 44:381-402.

Casselton, A.F. "Christian Enlightenment in Feofan Prokopovich's Tragicomedy 'Vladimir.' " (M.A., Auckland, 1967).

Christian, R.F. "A Recently Discovered 17th-Century Russian Manuscript." *SEER* 46 (1968):195-209.

Čiževskij, Dmitrij. *History of Old Russian Literature: From the 11th to the 19th Century.* (SPR 12). The Hague: Mouton, 1958.

Della Cava, C.T. "Sermons of Feofan Prokopovič: Themes and Style." (Ph.D., Columbia, 1972).

Fennell, J.L.I. and A. Stokes. *Early Russian Literature.* Berkeley: U. of California Press, 1974.

Gudzy, N.K. *History of Early Russian Literature,* trans. from 2nd Russian edition by Susan Wilbur Jones. Intro. by Gleb Struve. New York, 1949. Review: Posin, J.A. *RusR* 8:351-3.

Harkins, William Edward. "The Mythic Element in the *Tale of Gore-Zločastie.*" *For Roman Jakobson,* pp. 200-206.

Harkins, William Edward. "The Pathetic Hero in Russian Seventeenth Century Literature." *ASEER* 14:512-527.

Harkins, William Edward. "Russian Folk Ballads and the *Tale of Misery and Ill Fortune.*" *ASEER* 13:402-13.

Hippisley, Anthony. "The Emblem in the Writings of Simeon Polotsky." *SEEJ* 15:167-83.

Lewitter, L.R. "A Study of the Academic Drama in Russia and the Ukraine in the Seventeenth and Eighteenth Centuries, with Special Reference to its Polish Origins." (Ph.D., Cambridge, 1950).

Marshall, Richard H. "The Seventeenth-Century Popular 'Satires': Annotated Translations and a Survey of Critical Approaches." *DAI* 33: 5686A (Columbia).

Mirsky, D.S. *A History of Russian Literature,* edited and abridged by Francis J. Whitfield. New York: Knopf, 1949. 518 pp.

Šerech, J. "On Feofan Prokopovič as Writer and Preacher in His Kiev Period." HSS 2(1954):211-24.

Šerech, J. "Stefan Yavorsky and the Conflict of Ideologies in the Age of Peter I." *SEER* 30(1951):40-62.

Simmons, R.W., Jr. "Some Notes on Comparative Drama in the Seventeenth and Eighteenth Centuries: Russian, Polish, and German." *ThR* 2(1964): 13-17.

Slonim, Marc L'vovich. *The Epic of Russian Literature. From its Origins through Tolstoy.* New York: Oxford U.P., 1950. 367 pp.

Slonim, Marc L'vovich. *Russian Theatre from the Empire to the Soviets.* New York: World, 1961. 354 pp.

Stokes, A.D. "Literature, from the Beginning to 1700." *YWMLS* 24(for 1964):669-74.

Stone, John A. "The Pastor and the Tzar: A Comment on *The Comedy of Artaxerxes." BNYPL* 72:215-51.

Varneke, Boris V. *History of the Russian Theatre (Seventeenth Through Nineteenth Century).* Original trans. by Boris Brasol, rev. and ed. by Belle Martin. New York, 1951.

Waliszewski, K. *A History of Russian Literature.* New York and London: Appleton, 1900. 451 pp. Reprinted: New York: Kennikat, 1969.

Weiner, Jack. "The Death of Philip IV of Spain and the Early Russian Theatrical Repertoire." *ThR* 10(1970):179-85.

Wiener, Leo. *Anthology of Russian Literature.* New York: Putnam, 1902-03. Vol. 1. 447 pp. Reprinted New York: Benjamin Blom, 1967.

Zenkovsky, Serge A., ed. and tr. *Medieval Russia's Epics, Chronicles, and Tales.* New York: Dutton, 1963.

Zenkovsky, Serge A. "The Old Believer Avvakum and His Role in Russian Literature." *ISS* 1:1-56.

INDEX

accent (in verse) 98, 100
"Account of the Battle with Mamay" 16
acrostic 101, 102, 105, 108, 117
"Acrostic Alphabet" 107
Adrian, Patriarch of Moscow (d. 1700)
111, 112, 113, 115
Adrianova-Peretts, Varvara P. 57, 123
Aelian (Claudius Aelianus: fl. late 2nd-
early 3rd cent. A.D.) 118
Aesop (6th cent. B.C.?)
"Fables" 25
Alaric the Visigoth (d. 410) 131, 139
Alexander the Great, King of Macedon
(356-323 B.C.) 26
Alexander Nevsky, Prince of Novgorod
(1252-1263) 43
Alexandrine line 98
Alexei Alexeevich Romanov, tsarevich
(d. 1676) 110, 111
Alexei Mikhailovich Romanov (tsar
1645-1676) 4, 5, 23, 29, 52, 55, 61,
62, 63, 64, 66, 78, 106, 110, 111,
118, 144, 146
Alexei Petrovich Romanov, tsarevich
(d. 1718) 112, 115, 123, 156
allegorical characters (in drama) 144,
146, 149
"Alyosha and Tugarin Zmeevich" 81
Alyosha Popovich, bogatyr 79, 81
anisosyllabism 100, 102, 103, 107
"Annalistic Book" (1626): see Katy-
ryov-Rostovsky
Antoninus, Marcus Bassianus "Caracalla,"
Roman Emperor A.D. 211-217 139
"Apollonius of Tyre" 10
Apuleius, Lucius of Madaura (2nd cent.
A.D.) 20
Arion (late 7th cent. B.C.) 118
Ariosto, Ludovico (1474-1533) 3
Arnold, Matthew (1822-1888)
Sohrab and Rustem 48
assonance 76, 98
Aubigné, Théodore Agrippa d' (1551-
1630) 139
Augustine, Saint (Aurelius Augustinus,
A.D. 354-430)
["God-Seen Love"] 123
Augustus Caesar, Roman Emperor (43
B.C.-A.D. 14) 4
autobiography 41, 61, 67, 72
Avars 11

Avvakum Petrovich, Archpriest (1621-
1682) 8, 41, 61-72
Life of Avvakum Written by Himself
8, 54, 61-72, 159, 160

Balde, Jakob (1604-1668)
*De Vanitate Mundi (On the Vanity of
the World)* 130, 138
Baratynsky, Eugene Abramovich (1800-
1844) 160
Baroque 7, 38, 39, 40, 69, 129, 130
"Basil Golden-Hair" 10
Bebel, Heinrich (1472-1518)
Facetiae 25
Belobotsky, Andrei [Jan Bielobocki]
(d. early 1700s) 109, 113, 114, 129-
139, 159
Pentateugum ("Five Books") 117,
129-139
Belorussia 99, 102, 103, 109, 116, 143,
144, 145, 149
Bernini, Giovanni Lorenzo (1598-1680)
"Ecstasy of Saint Teresa" 38
"Beuve d'Antone" 46
"Bevis of Hampton" 10, 46
Bible
Apocalypse 131, 134, 137
Daniel 145
Ecclesiastes 106
Esther 147
Genesis 87, 90
Gospels 135
Judith (Apocrypha) 147
Psalms 108
Bolotnikov, Ivan 76
Boniface VIII, Pope (1294-1303) 63
Boris and Gleb, Saints: sons of St. Vla-
dimir 151
Bracciolini-Poggio, Gian Francesco
(1380-1459)
Facetiae 25
Brahms, Johannes (1833-1897) 118
"The Brightly Shining Star" (*Presvet-
laia zvezda*) 9, 25
Brudecki, Zygmunt 130, 131, 138
"Cztery rzeczy człowieku ostateczne"
138
"bureaucrat school" (*Prikaznaia Shkola*)
105, 107, 108
bylina 5, 10, 78-81, 87, 91
bylina verse 80, 86, 87, 100

175

Byzantium, Byzantine 3, 7, 11, 41, 62, 63, 100, 101, 102, 116, 143, 144

Caesar, Gaius Julius (100-44 B.C.) 138
caesura 116, 117, 120, 130
Calderón de la Barca, Pedro (1600-1681) 159
  Devotion to the Cross 38
Catherine II, "the Great," Empress (1762-1796) 79
Catullus, Gaius Valerius (c. 84-c. 54 B.C.) 118
Cerularius, Michael, Patriarch of Constantinople (1053-1058) 63
Cervantes, Miguel Saavedra de (1547-1616) 3, 6, 159
Charlemagne, King of the Franks 768-814 79
Charles XII, King of Sweden 1682-1718 128
Chet'ii Minei: see Makarios, Metropolitan
chivalric novella (tale) 10, 45-50, 80
chronicle *(letopis')* 8, 10, 12, 13, 37
"Chronicle of 1606": see "Other Relation"
"Chronograph" 11
Chulkov, Mikhail Dmitrievich (1743-1793)
  The Comely Cook 160
Cicero, Marcus Tullius (106-43 B.C.) 118
classicism 7, 9, 38, 40
Colonne, Guido delle (c. 1215-c. 1290)
  Historia destructionis Troiae 17, 19, 20
"Comedy of Judith": see Gregorii, Johann Gottfried
compilation 9, 10, 23, 25, 37
congratulatory verses 117, 121, 123
Corneille, Pierre (1606-1684) 6, 159
Counter-Reformation 7
court literature 38, 39

Danilov, V.V. 84
Dante Alighieri (1265-1321) 136, 137
Daphni 121
"Deeds of the Romans" *(Rimskie deianiia)* 9, 24
"democratic verse" 6, 8, 75, 97, 103
Demosthenes (384-322 B.C.) 118
Derzhavin, Gavriil Romanovich (1743-1816) 160
Dimitry Ivanovich, son of Ivan IV (1581-1591) 4

Dimitry Tuptalo of Rostov (Saint Dimitry Rostovsky) (1651-1709) 99, 109, 114, 115, 125, 127, 148, 149, 150
  "Ascension of the Virgin" 149
  "Birth of Christ" 149
  Chet'ii Minei 115, 127, 149
  "Resurrection of Christ" 149
  "Song to St. Demetrius of Thessalonica" 127
Dmitriev, Lev Alexandrovich 30, 32
Dolgoruky, Mikhail Yurevich 114
"Domostroi": see Sylvester, Archpriest
Donne, John (1572-1631) 39, 129, 159
Dostoevsky, Fyodor Mikhailovich (1821-1881) 159
  Notes from Underground 92, 160
double words 87
drama 9, 118, 143-156, 159
Druzhina-Ozor'in, Kallistrat
  "Life of Saint Juliania Lazarevskaya" 9, 28, 29, 30

elegy 9
emblematic verses 117, 123
"English players" 145
entertainment literature 80, 81
Epifany, monk
  Life of Epifany 72
epigram 117
epistle, verse 105, 107, 117
"Epistle of One Nobleman to Another" 76-78, 103
epitaph 107, 108, 117, 121
euphuism 39
Evstraty 103, 104
  "Tale of a Certain Contention" 104
exemplary tale 41
exemplum 23, 138

"Fable of the Drunkard" 60
"Fable of the Fox and the Cock" 60
"Fable of the Old Husband" 60
"False-Dimitry I" ("Grishka Otrepev Rostriga"), tsar 1606 4, 12, 14, 17, 18, 19, 20, 21, 84, 104
"False-Dimitry II" ("Brigand of Tushino": d. 1610) 4, 19, 22
Farsit, Hugues
  Miracula virginis (12th cent.) 25
"Fatsetsii" 25
Faust legend 42, 43
feet (metrical) 97, 98
Feodor I Ivanovich, tsar 1584-1598: 4, 12

Feodor II Alexeevich Romanov, tsar
  1676-1682 5, 66, 107, 110, 111,
  112, 113, 114
Filaret (Feodor Nikitich Romanov),
  Patriarch (d. 1633) 5, 12, 82
Filofei, monk (fl. c. 1510)
  "doctrine of the three Romes" 3, 64
Firdausi, Abu'l Qasim (941-1019)
  Shah-Nameh 48
folklore literature 22, 38, 45, 46, 49,
  75-76
folk song 10
Fonvizin, Denis Ivanovich (1745-1792)
  The Minor 160
free accent 98
Frischlin, Philipp Nicodemus (1547-
  1590) 25
Funikov, Ivanets 76-77

Gardie, Jacques de la 22
Gautama Buddha 120
genres, medieval 3-33, 37
genres, modern 9, 37-72
Georgios Hamartolos (9th cent.) 11
German, monk (d. 1682)· 107
Gesta Romanorum 10, 24
Godunov, Boris, tsar 1584-1605 4, 11,
  12, 17, 18, 83, 84
Godunova, Xenia Borisovna, daughter of
  Boris Godunov 19, 20, 83, 85
Goethe, Johann Wolfgang von (1749-
  1832) 145
  Faust 90
Golitsyn, Prince Vasily V. 110, 112, 123
Golosov, Lukian, *dimnii diak* 113
Goncharov, Ivan Alexandrovich (1812-
  1891) 159
Gongora y Argote, Luis (1561-1627)
  129, 159
  Soledades 39
Gorfunkel, A. 129, 130, 132
"Gorgianic figures" 103
Gothic style 37, 40
Government Printing Office (*Pechatnyi
  dvor*) 105, 112
Gramman, Dr. Hartmann 106
"The Great Mirror" 9, 23
El Greco (Domenico Theotocopuli) (c.
  1598-1625)
  "St. Martin and the Beggar" 39
Gregory, Johann Gottfried (d. 1675)
  144, 146, 147, 148
  "Artaxerxes Action" 147

Gregory (cont).
  "Comedy of Judith" 9, 147-148
  "The Lamentable Story of Adam and
    Eve" 147
  "Small Entertaining Comedy of
    Joseph" 147
  "Tobias the Younger" 147
Griboedov, Alexander Sergeevich (1795-
  1829)
Grimmelshausen, Johann Jakob Chris-
  toph von (1622-1676)
  Simplicissimus 51
Gryphius, Andreas (1616-1664) 139
Gusev, V.E. 68, 71

Hapsburgs 4
Hannibal (247-183 B.C.) 132
Herodotus (490/480-430/425 B.C.) 90
heroic poem 123
"Hildebrandslied" 48
historical memoir 10
historical romance 43
historical song 80
Historiye Rzymskie 24
history 11, 13
"Holiday Mass of the Tavern Idlers" 58
Homer 118
homily 68
Huns 11
hymn 102, 107, 108
hymn, Latin 100, 116
  "Ut queant laxis resonare fibris"
    (Guido of Arezzo) 118
  "Pange, lingua, gloriosi proelium cer-
    taminis" (Sedulius) 120

Ilya Muromets, bogatyr 79, 81
interlude 145, 149
Ioachim, Patriarch of Moscow (d. 1690)
  111, 112, 114
Ioanniky, deacon 107
Iosif, Patriarch of Moscow (d. 1652) 63
Isaiia, abbot 31
isosyllabism 102, 108, 116
Istomin, Karion [Zaulonsky] (c. 1650-
  1717) 109, 112, 113, 116, 123-127,
  129
  versified "Domostroi" 117, 123-125
  "Epistle to Dimitry Tuptalo" 125
  "How Monks live in the Monastery"
    126
Ivan III, tsar 1462-1505 3
Ivan IV "the Terrible," tsar 1530-1584

Ivan IV (cont.)
  4, 7, 8, 13, 19, 20, 65, 79, 80, 123
  "Letters to Prince Andrei Kurbsky"
    19
Ivan V Alexeevich Romanov, tsar 1682-
  1696 5, 110, 111
"Ivan Godinovich" 81

Jack Wilton, or The Unfortunate Travel-
  ler: see Nashe, Thomas
James, Richard 82, 86
Jesuit school drama 144, 152
Jonson, Ben (1572-1637) 159
Josephus, Flavius (37/38-c. 100) 26
  Jewish Wars 16, 18
Jovian, Roman Emperor 24

Kantemir, Antiokh Dmitrievich (1709-
  1744) 5, 99, 155
Kapnist, Vasily Vasilievich (1757-1824)
  Yabeda 160
Karamzin, Nikolai Mikhailovich (1766-
  1826) 80
Katyryov-Rostovsky, Prince Ivan Mikhai-
  lovich (d. 1640) 8, 11, 18, 20, 21
  "The Annalistic Book" 12, 17, 100,
    102
  virshi 17, 100
Kazi-Griey, Khan of the Crimea 82
Khristos paskhon 143
Khvorostinin, Ivan Andreevich (d. 1625)
  76, 103, 104
  "Prayer to Christ" 105
King Arthur 79
Kochanowski, Jan (1530-1584) 99
Kubasov, Sergei 11
Kuhlmann, Quirinus (1651-1689) 139
Kurbsky, Prince Andrei Mikhailovich
  (1528?-1583) 4, 7, 19
Kvashnin, Peter Andreevich 84, 86

La Fontaine, Jean de (1621-1695) 159
lamentation 83, 117
"Lamentation over the Conquest and
  Total Destruction . . . of the Musco-
  vite State" 16
Latin-Greek-Slavonic Academy 114
Lazarillo de Tormes 51
learned poetry 80, 97-139
"Legend of the Peasant's Son" 58
Lermontov, Mikhail Yurevich (1814-
  1841) 159, 160
Lesage, Alain René (1668-1747)

Lesage (cont.)
  Gil-Blas de Santillane 51
"Life of Alexander Nevsky" 16
The Life of Archpriest Avvakum, Writ-
  ten by Himself: see Avvakum
"Life of the Boyarina Morozova, Prin-
  cess Urusova and Maria Danilova" 29
"Life of Juliania Lazarevskaya": see
  Druzhina-Ozorin, Kallistrat
"Life of Peter and Fevronia" 28
"Life of Saints Boris and Gleb" 26
Likhachev, Dmitry Sergeevich 6, 7, 26,
  27, 28, 37, 39, 40, 57, 61
Likhudy brothers 114, 116
"literary etiquette" 9, 16, 27
literary system 9, 13
literary trend 28, 40
Lomonosov, Mikhail Vasilievich (1711-
  1765) 5, 39, 118, 160
"Lord Novgorod the Great" 79
Lucan (Marcus Annaeus Lucanus, A.D.
  39-65)
  Pharsalia 138
Lucullus, Lucius Licinius, Roman con-
  sul 71 B.C. 139
Lull, Ramón (1235-1315) 114
  Ars brevis 114
  Ars magna 114
  Rhetorica 114
lyric verse 82, 86, 87, 100

Makarios, Metropolitan (1528-1563) 16
  Chet'ii minei 23
Malalas, John (491?-578?) 11
Markovna, Nastasya, wife of Archpriest
  Avvakum 71, 72
Marlowe, Christopher (1563/4-1593)
  The Tragicall History of Dr. Faustus
    145
  Tamburlaine the Great 149
Mazeppa, Ivan, Hetman of the Ukraine
  (1644-1709) 128, 152
"Medical Handbook on How to Treat
  Foreigners" 58
Medvedev, Sylvester [Semen Agafoniko-
  vich Medvedev] (1641-1691) 109,
  111, 112, 113, 114, 116, 117, 120-
  122, 123, 159
  Epitafion 121
  "Greeting to the Tsarevna Sophia"
    121
  "Verses for Holy Saturday" 122
Melander 25

Mikhail Fyodorovich Romanov, Tsar
  1613-1645 5, 12, 13, 14, 82
"Mikhailo Potok" 79, 81
Miloslavskaya, Maria, Tsaritsa 1648-
  1669 110
Milton, John (1608-1674) 6, 159
Mogila Academy of Kiev 63, 111, 114,
  115, 150, 156
Molière, Jean-Baptiste Poquelin de (1622-
  1673) 159
Molina, Tirso de [pseudonym of Gabriel
  Tellez] (1571?-1648) 159
Mongols: see Tatars
morality play 144
Morozova, Boyarina 65
Mstislavsky, Fyodor Ivanovich 18
music, church 107

Naryshkina, Natalia, Tsaritsa (1671-
  1694) 110, 111, 112
Nasedka, Ivan 103
  "Statement Against the Lutherans"
  104
Nash, Ogden (1902-   ) 100
Nashe, Thomas (1567-1601)
  Jack Wilton, or The Unfortunate
  Traveller 51
Nebuchadnezzar, King of Babylon (605-
  562 B.C.) 24, 131
negative comparison 81, 82, 85
Nerchinsk, Treaty of (1689) 114
Nerezi 122
Nero, Roman Emperor A.D. 54-68 139
Neronov, Ivan, Archpriest 62, 64
Nestor, Monk (11th-early 12th cent.) 8,
  11
New Jerusalem Monastery 63, 107, 108,
  116
"New Tale of the Illustrious Russian
  Tsardom and Great State of
  Muscovy" (1610) 12
Niess, Johann 130, 138
  author of last two cantos of *Quat-*
  tuor hominis ultima
Nikitichi-Yurevye (Romanovy) 14
Nikon, Patriarch (1652-1660) 62-63,
  64, 66, 68, 69, 107
novel 68, 71
novel, historical 9, 43
Novodevichy Convent 111

ode 117, 118, 121, 128
"Old Ritualists" ("Old Believers") 29,

"Old Ritualists" (cont.)
  41, 61, 64, 72
Olearius, Adam (c. 1599-1671) 106
oral literature 5, 41, 75, 80, 97
Ordyn-Nashchokin, Afanasy Lavren-
  tievich 51, 146
"Other Relation" (1606) 12, 16
Otrepev, Grigory (Grishka): see False-
  Dimitry I
Ovid (Publius Ovidius Naso, 43 B.C.-
  A.D. 17) 118

Palytsyn, Avraamy (c. 1555-1627) 8,
  12, 17, 102
  "Relation" *(Skazanie)* 13, 14, 15, 16
Panchenko, Alexander Mikhailovich 21,
  100, 102, 105, 109, 117, 123, 127
parallelism (in verse) 97
paraphrase of Psalms 117, 127
parody 41, 55
Pashkov, Governor 67, 71
Paul of Aleppo 124, 125
Pazukhin, S.I. 86
peasantry *(krestianstvo)* 62, 65
Pechenegs 11, 79
Peretts, V.N. 103
"period style" 37, 40
periodization 6
Peter I (Peter Alexeevich Romanov),
  Tsar and Emperor, 1682-1725
  5, 6, 61, 110, 111, 112, 115, 116,
  128, 154, 156
"Peter of the Golden Keys" 10, 49
"Petition of the Kalyazin Monastery" 58
Petrus Alfonsi (11th cent.)
  Disciplina clericalis 24
Philotheos Kokkinos, Patriarch of Con-
  stantinople (1353-55; 1364-76) 101
picaresca (picaresque novel) 41, 51
picaresque tale 9, 50-54
Pickelhäring, German buffoon character
  145, 148
"Pierre et Magelone" 49
Plautus, Titus Maccius (before 251-184
  B.C.) 144
Pliny the Elder (Gaius Plinius Secundus,
  A.D. 23 or 24-79) 118
Polotsky, Simeon (1629-1680) 8, 84,
  93, 99, 109, 111, 112, 116, 117-120,
  121, 129, 134, 144, 148
  "The Carefree Debtor" 117
  "Comedy on Nebuchadnezzar" 118,
  145, 146
  "Comedy of the Prodigal Son" 118,

Polotsky, Simeon (cont.)
"Comedy of Prodigal Son" (cont.) 145, 146
"Garden of Many Flowers" 117, 118
"Prayer of Saint Ioasaph" 120
Ritmologion (Rifmologion) 118, 146
The Rod of Governance 117
"The Russian Eagle" 118, 131
Spiritual Dinner 117
Spiritual Supper 117
Polovtsy 11, 79
Pompey (Gnaeus Pompeius Magnus, 107-49 B.C.) 138
Pozharsky, Prince Dimitry 103
préciosité 39
"pre-Renaissance" 39
pre-syllabic verse 21, 75, 76, 99-103, 104-109
Prokhorov, G.M. 101
Prokopovich, Feofan (1681-1736) 99, 115
Tragicomedy of St. Vladimir 150-56
prose romance 41
Pushkin, Alexander Sergeevich (1799-1837) 46, 159, 160
Eugene Onegin 8, 160
Ruslan and Lyudmila 49

quantity (in verse) 97, 100
Quattuor himinis ultima: see Rader and Niess

Racine, Jean (1639-1699) 6, 59
Phèdre 155
Tite et Bérénice 155
Rader 130, 138
author of first two cantos of *Quattuor hominis ultima*
raek, raeshnyi verse 10, 75-78, 100, 103
Razin, Stepan, rebel and pirate 62
realism 6, 7, 40, 41
Reformation 7
Rej, Mikolaj (1505-1569) 99
"Relation" *(Skazanie)*: see Palitsyn, Avraamy
Renaissance 3, 7, 8, 38, 39, 40, 99, 143, 144, 145
retardation 81
"Reynard the Fox" 57
rhyme (in verse) 76, 93, 98, 100, 102, 108, 116, 130, 155
masculine rhyme 98, 99, 132

rhyme (in verse) (cont.)
feminine rhyme 98, 99, 116, 132
rhyming prose 13, 20, 102
rhythmic prose 75
Rilke, Rainer Maria (1875-1926) 160
Romanchukov, Alexei Savvich 106
Romanesque style 37, 40
Romanos the "Melodos" (fl. 5th-6th cent.)
"Hymn on the Resurrection" 101
romanticism 7, 9, 40
Ronsard, Pierre (1524/5-1585) 4
Rymsha, Andrei
"Apostol" 102
Ryurik, Prince of Novgorod (after 862) 4

saga 50
"Saga of Burnt-Njal" 50-51
saint's life *(zhitie)* 9, 22, 26, 37, 67, 68, 72
Samsonov, Peter 106
Sapphic strophe 116, 118, 119
satirical tale 41, 54
Savvaty, elder 13
Savvaty, Saint 30, 32
Savvaty, *spravchik* 105
schism (Raskol) 64, 65, 66, 72
"Second Shepherds' Play" (Wakefield cycle) 149
Semeon, Archbishop of Smolensk 113, 114
Seneca, Lucius Annaeus (c. 4 B.C.-A.D. 65) 144, 152
Sergius of Radonezh, Saint 14
serpentine verse 104
Severus, Septimius: Roman Emperor A.D. 193-211 139
Shakespeare, William (1564-1616) 3, 6, 159
Shakhovskoi, Semeon Ivanovich
"Epistle" 103, 104
Shein, General 43
Shemyaka, Dimitry 59
"Shemyaka's Judgment" 54, 58
Sheptaev, L.S. 84
Shuisky, Prince Dmitry Ivanovich 18
Shuisky, Vasily (tsar 1606-1610) 4, 12, 13, 17, 22, 77, 104
Sigismund III, King of Poland (1587-1632) 12, 14
Simplicissimus: see Grimmelshausen, Johann

skazka (fairy-tale) 91
skomorokh 76, 103
Skopin-Shuisky, Prince Mikhail Vasilie- vich (1586-1610) 22, 83
Skulsky, Andrei 143, 144
Skuratov, Malyuta 22
Skuratova, Princess Maria 22
Slavic languages
    Church Slavonic 100, 101, 148, 155, 159
    East Slavic 99
    Proto-Slavic 98
    South Slavic 99
    West Slavic 99
Smotritsky, Gerasim 102, 103
smuta (Time of Troubles) 4, 8, 12, 13, 17, 22, 42
Socialist realism 6
"Sohrab and Rustem": see Arnold, Matthew
Solovetsky Monastery 12, 13, 28, 30, 32
"Song of Igor's Campaign" (Slovo o polku Igoreve) 10, 82
Sophia Alexeevna Romanova (regent 1682-1689) 5, 110, 111, 112, 114, 123
"Spectacle of Human Life" (Zrelishche zhitiia chelovecheskogo) (1675) 25
Speculum magnum exemplorum (15th cent.) 23, 24
Speransky, M.N. 84
"Spiritual Regulation" 156
spiritual song (kant) 116, 127
Stabreim 97
standard (constant) epithet 81, 87
Sumorokov, Alexander Petrovich (1718-1777) 5, 155
syllabic verse 10, 75, 86, 97-103, 107, 109-139, 144
syllabo-tonic verse 98
Sylvester, Archpriest 123
    "Domostroi"?
symbolism (Decadence) 6, 40

"Tale of Bova Korolevich" 10, 45-47, 80
"Tale of the Capital Kiev and the Russian Bogatyrs" 79
"Tale of the Death and Burial of Prince Mikhailo Skopin-Shuisky" 22
"Tale of Eruslan (Uruslan) Lazarevich" 45, 47-50, 80
"Tale of the Founding of the Page's

Monastery of Tver" 43-45
"The Tale of Frol Skobeev" 9, 50-54, 57, 61, 159
"The Tale of Karp Sutulov" 54
"Tale of the Kiev Bogatyrs" 80, 81
"Tale of Melusine" 49
"Tale of the Roman Emperor Otto" 49
"The Tale of Savva Grudtsyn" 41-43
"The Tale of Sorrow-Misfortune" 54, 87-93, 97, 159, 160
"Tale of Varlaam and Ioasaph" 120
"The Tale of Yorsh Yorshevich" 54-57, 58
    "Yorsh Yorshevich" (rhymed) 57
Tatars (Mongols, Golden Horde) 3, 4, 79, 110
"Temir-Aksakevo Deistvo" 149
Terence (Publius Terentius Afer) (195?-159 B.C.) 144
Thomas à Kempis (c. 1380-1471)
    Imitatio Christi 114
"three Romes," doctrine of: see Filofei, monk
Tikhon, Archimandrite 107
Titus Flavius: Roman Emperor A.D. 79-81: 139
Tolstoi, Lev Nikolaevich (1828-1910) 159
tragicomedy 150, 151
Trajan, Roman Emperor 98-117 139
transsubstantiation 112, 114
Trediakovsky, Vasily Kirillovich (1703-1769) 5, 39, 118
Trinity Monastery of St. Sergius 12, 13, 16, 111
Turgenev, Ivan Sergeevich (1818-1883) 72, 159
Tyutchev, Fyodor Ivanovich (1803-1873) 160

Ukraine, Ukrainian 4, 6, 62, 99, 102, 103, 107, 111, 116, 149, 152, 155
Ulozhenie (law code) of Alexei Mikhailovich (1649) 55, 62
Union of Brest (1595) 62
Urusova, Boyarina 66

Vasily II Vasilevich "the Dark," Tsar 1425-1462 59
Vasily, monk 107
Vassian, abbot 13
Vega Carpio, Lope Félix de (1562-1635) 6

181

verse 10, 13, 20, 38
Vincent de Beauvais (c. 1190-1264) 118
   Speculum magnum 10
Virgil (Publius Vergilius Maro, 70-19
   B.C.) 118
Vladimir Monomakh (Grand Duke of
   Kiev 1113-1125) 8, 79
   "Testament" 41, 61
Vladimir I Svyatoslavovich, Saint (Grand
   Prince of Kiev 973-1015) 63, 79,
   151
Vladislav Zhigmontov (i.e. Vladislav, son
   of Sigismund III, King of Poland) 13
Vodovozov, N.V. 78
Volkovich, Ioanniky 143, 144
Vortynsky, I.M. 22

Wielkie Zwierciadło przykładów 23

Xenia, Grand Princess of Vladimir 44

Yaropolk Svyatoslavovich, brother of
   Vladimir the Saint 151
Yaroslav Yaroslavych, Grand Duke of
   Vladimir (1263-1276) 43, 44
Yavorsky, Stefan (1658-1722) 99, 109,
   115, 127, 128, 156
   "Mother Russia to the Traitor Ma-
   zeppa" 128
   "To His Library" 115, 128

Zaikonospassky Monastery school 111,
   112, 117
"zealots for piety" 62, 63, 64
Zlobin, Mikhail 106
Zosima, Saint 30, 32